Sex and the Sober Alcoholic

— a healing guide and workbook

by *Toby Rice Drews*

Recovery Communications, Inc.
P.O. Box 19910
Baltimore, MD 21211
(301) 243-8558

ISBN # 0-9615995-0-2

Library of Congress # 87-062046

First Printing: January, 1988
Recovery Communications, Inc.
P.O. Box 19910
Baltimore, MD 21211
(301) 243-8558

Contents

OTHER BOOKS BY TOBY RICE DREWS:

GETTING YOUR CHILDREN SOBER
LIGHT THIS DAY! (Daily Meditations/Daily Journal)
GETTING THEM SOBER, VOLUME ONE
GETTING THEM SOBER, VOLUME TWO
GETTING THEM SOBER, VOLUME THREE
GET RID OF ANXIETY AND STRESS

Introduction

Sex is basically what goes on between the ears. And in that sense, alcoholics are confused and conflicted people.

We're wanters. We want. Then we get. Then we're bored. We go on to the next. We feel guilty. We stop. We get depressed. We want some more, but this time we can't get. We're resentful. We feel guilty again. We get angry because we feel guilty.

And, all of this in one week!

A recovered alcoholic who was single and sexually active, may have a sponsor who has been monogamous and married all through his/her active addiction. That sponsor is likely to say, kindly but in a bewildered manner, "Pray about it, and don't take the first drink."

You don't drink.

But you still feel alone.

Psychiatrists often don't understand alcoholics, nor do they understand their important need to be rigid about what they can and cannot do, to maintain sobriety...especially in its early stages. This rigidity can also induce too much guilt, too much resentment, or bring on emotional isolation. We cannot afford too much isolation, too long, because we are only as sick as our secrets.

This book, then, is an attempt to assist the sober alcoholic and his/her family in the areas of sexuality, not by teaching or preaching, but by power of example.

Alcoholics do not respond well to people telling them what to do, or what not to do. They react best to more-experienced recovering alcoholics telling them what they've been through, how they handled it — well or badly — and how they stayed sober through it all.

They talk through the pain of having to say no, and the pain of having to say yes. Then comes the most excruciating pain of all, the one alcoholics know only too well, the pain of not getting their way.

As I conducted the interviews that form the basis for this book, I became aware of a very interesting question which has become the underlying theme of the book: OLD-FASHIONED MORALITY vs. SITUATIONAL ETHICS, or has guilt really lessened since the 1940s —at least, for alcoholics?

Bill Wilson, one of the founders of Alcoholics Anonymous, wrote, "We've had more than our fair share of romance."

Indeed!

We are really very, very straight people. We may have seemed wild in our drinking days, but in reality, our value systems are quite Victorian.

Even the cynics among us love to be swept off their feet by the stories and miracles we not only hear, but witness daily, in treatment programs.

We are so sensitive to the pain we hear.

A woman with three years of sobriety is still very depressed because she's so lonely. She tells only her best friend, after meetings, how she wishes she could begin again to trust. But she's afraid to step out and have any kind of sexual relationship. She's been burned so badly in the past. She's so afraid she could not go through being burned again, and stay sober at the same time.

We all go through such "pullings." It doesn't seem to matter about our religious or ethnic backgrounds, we are mostly so very straight! We acted out all the sexual "liberation" ideas, but can we handle it, sober? You may not believe that the drinking, the alcoholism, is at all connected to this pulling — but it is. We don't often know it until "the fog clears," that is, until you've had a year or two of sobriety. Then you find yourself starting to identify with others in treatment groups and saying, "Oh, my God, I really did feel that way!"

Alcoholism is the only disease that tells you that you don't have it. Thirty out of thirty-five alcoholics never even reach treatment because they don't believe they have a problem with alcohol and/or pills.

We take a pill or a drink to "calm down." We don't know when our speech is slurred. Families and colleagues are usually too embarrassed to tell us, because they respect us; we're often professionals.

We all say it's a disease; but, we often believe it's a shame.

We won't like others if they tell us about our behavior.

So, they don't tell us.

The paradox is that all the depressed feelings, all the anxiety that we drink or pill over, becomes accentuated, and then activated, by that very same booze and/or pills — and we don't even know it. So we take a little bit more each time; but it's such a small increase that it goes unnoticed again. We are aware, though, that it is taking more time for the drink or pill to take the desired effect.

That's addiction. And addiction colors everything, including our sex lives.

We become bored, depressed, more bored, more depressed. It takes more travel, more partners, more running, more stimulation for us to feel good. MORE of everything! And then, the good feeling quickly dissipates.

As the disease progresses, we may find ourselves acting out sexually with people we would never normally be involved with. People we wouldn't find attractive if we were sober — people we might even pity.

Alcoholism makes the pain stay. It makes us obsess with the loneliness, with the existential pain. We revel in the *angst*; we rationalize that it makes us interesting. Addiction makes us lie to ourselves, that "we don't have an alcohol or pill problem." That we have "psychiatric problems" instead. It makes excited misery and obsession a way of life.

* * * * * * *

The sometimes agonizing choices of alcoholics and their families —subjects that are not often spoken about, except in whispers — are what this book is about.

I've interviewed people who are struggling to be comfortable without injuring others. And in situations where others are injured — sometimes it was unavoidable — especially where *any* answer would bring pain.

These are the common problems I discovered: How to get through the first year of sobriety, when your sponsor warns that new relationships are unwise, right now — without falling into self-pity. How to get through the next year's E.S.I. (Early Sobriety Insanity) of poor choices. How to handle the mid-life sobriety crisis that long-term sober people often face.

Then there are the problems of withdrawal... hormones...a foggy head...and the erroneous idea that one is well when one *isn't*, yet.

And families and amends and lust and depression.

I felt that this book was unavoidable. Almost no area of sober life is as difficult as the sexual one. Alcoholics and their families are probably the most all-or-nothing, the most sensitive, the most easily bored, and the most easily stimulated persons on this earth.

Dear Lord, Thank you for helping me in the process of my recovery. Lead me and my family into wholeness in every area of our lives. Teach me to face the issues surrounding my sexuality with your grace and truth. As your light shines on my areas of need, help me to surrender them to your workmanship. Amen

Is Sober-Sex Terrifying?

"The Lord is my light and my salvation — whom shall I fear? The Lord is the stronghold of my life —of whom shall I be afraid" (Ps. 27:1).

1

For many, the prospect of having a sexual relationship with a finally sober spouse is lovely. And the reality is, that for many spouses, it does become a wonderful part of life, with the former ugliness a thing of the past.

For other families, however, and for many alcoholics, the prospect of sexuality in a sober context is frightening.

"Where's the excitement that alcohol brings on?" "I can't face *anything* sober!" "I'm too shy, sober." "I've always had sex with a drinking wife. Won't she be too *aware*, sober?"

These fears sometimes get talked about; often, however, they're only whispered. Many times, they remain unexpressed, because of accompanying feelings of shame, isolation and embarrassment. Spouses, even after fifteen or more years of marriage, often can't voice these most intimate of feelings because they are afraid of being rejected or put down if they say such things out loud. Alcoholics who are newly sober often don't know exactly *what* they're afraid of. Their fears mesh with the toxic-fears of early sobriety into one 'big lump.'

The following stories were told to me by recovering alcoholics and their families who have gotten through these fears. They went through the process, but not usually unpainfully!

They learned to talk to God, themselves and another human being about what bothered them — even when they felt embarrassed.

*   *   *   *   *   *   *

"Part of my fears about having sober sex concerned my 'getting older and whether I'd still be attractive.' I was only thirty when I got sober, and I've been sober seventeen years, now. But I didn't see it then as 'only thirty years old' — I saw it as Oh, my God, I'm thirty! I knew that if I had been drinking, I could have momentarily forgotten it. But not so when I became sober. I had to deal with it — even if I had to be stark-raving sober about it!

"When I was drinking, I had visions of myself growing older and getting more and more anxious and needing to drink more and more, and trying to hide it, and slowly being more and more out of control — and not even seeing it in myself.

"I envisioned myself as desperate and staying in relationships with old 'interesting, late-stage alcoholics' who would be the only ones I could be with. And the drinking would increase; the sex would be minimal; and then, nothing.

"I know that most women who are still drinking and 'pill-ing' deny their alcoholism. They think of aging only in terms of fears of being elderly women. Somehow, I could not ignore my alcoholism. I constantly feared seeing myself as an aging-woman-alcoholic."

*   *   *   *   *   *   *

That was Maxine — "Max" to her friends. She was good-looking, athletic, auburn-haired and forty-seven years old. I was in Wyoming visiting friends, and I interviewed Max and several other recovered alcoholics who had been sober anywhere from three to thirty years each. All of them wanted to talk with me when I told them I was working on this book. Most people I encountered offered to give me interviews without even having to ask them. This book was different. This book allowed people to finally express what they've been holding in, not sharing, for years and years into their sobriety.

A lot of them said they saw it as an extension of their A.A. or Al-Anon "Fifth Step," a part of their healing process that involved sharing secrets, so they could fully join the human race and not hold back to protect a part of themselves they were still ashamed of.

*   *   *   *   *   *   *

"Max," of course, is not her real name. But the feelings are hers. And the freedom she realized by finally sharing is hers, definitely and permanently.

She went on, "Sober, I can be afraid of sex; I can be afraid of aging. But, I get a certain amount of acceptance about life. I don't *rage* about things I cannot change — at least, not for the length of time I used to.

"I learned to come to terms with my fears and not just ignore them. When I have a problem, there are certain things I've taught myself to do about it. One, I ask myself, is there anything at all I can do about it? If not, I have to live *through* it a day at a time, and I have to learn, a day at a time, what my fears are about the situation, and then I have to do something about those fears.

"One way to look at it is to continually tell myself that aging and sober sex are parts of life as it is supposed to be, and that it is just another chapter in my life. This puts my fears in perspective. *It's just another thing.*

"So, the alternative is to decide to go crazy about it —because I am an *extremely* defiant person! Or to become baby-ish; I want the world the way *I* want it! Or simply to accept it. You do as well as you can with that last one. It's not usually perfect acceptance at all! Whatever, wherever, you are at that time, you accept as much as you can. It's certainly better than it was."

Sarah, who had been quiet until now, finally felt comfortable enough to share her feelings:

"How was sober sex different? When I was drinking, I could feign naivete. I could pretend to men that it was all their idea. I could almost pretend it to myself. In my mind, I stayed innocent. I was the waif; the ephemeral sexy dancer-in-the-clouds, who went along with men, and had no responsibility for herself. Therefore, I could stay young and ageless. La-de-da, all the time! La-La land!

"Sober, there was no way I could say, 'I didn't know what I was *really* doing.' I saw reality. I saw myself. I saw my husband. I saw the grime in my house. I saw the grime in the bars. I saw the grime in my personality and in his. It was all very, very real.

"The very consciousness of it all brought on all the guilt and embarrassment I could never face, before.

"Sober, the decision is mixed up with what your and his value systems are. Drunk, it's such a shallow decision. I was single when I was still drinking. I chose a man because he seemed hip on the surface. Because he wore suits and had a briefcase and a good vocabulary, and was nice on two dates. Or one.

"You never asked the questions about nuances, and you never really looked at the cues he gave you. At least I didn't. I *saw* them. But I ignored them, if they would deny me the pleasure of the immediate moment, *or if they would make me not have a relationship with this man and fill an immediate bottomless-pit-need to be taken care of, emotionally.*

"Drunk, or drinking, I had too many starving emotional needs, panics, terrors. I needed to be taken care of. I needed a care-taker. Terribly needy people can't be choosy."

Sarah's whole body was more relaxed after talking with us. "I never told anyone any of this. I'm married now, and happy. And I have this self-image thing that I am the upright woman in the suburbs and church." She laughed, "I guess I still have some belief that everyone is what they *look* like. You know, the man in the suit is wonderful and his wife and kids never have a bad thought or feeling. And I'd never believe he used to beat her. And that she used to have affairs. Because they *look* wonderful!"

I found Sarah's expression to be an underlying theme in all the interviews. No matter how 'sophisticated' a person was, each one expressed some degree of wonder at the very humanness of others — underneath the image that belied anything other than Ozzie and Harriet!

Carla spoke: "When I was active in my addiction, I was going to do what I was going to do regardless of the consequences. It was like my home: I could not at all face cleaning my bathroom. So, when I got sober, the porcelain was all black. It had not been cleaned in three years. It's not that I didn't want a clean bathroom; I just had lost the capacity to deal with a growing number of issues, and the bathroom seemed like a big one.

"The same with consequences about sex. I could not function sexually, except as an animal. I went through the motions. But I only thought about my anxiety and how to alleviate it. It consumed me; I was in such pain. I guess I thought sex was a diversion. But it left me with depression and more pills."

Sheila, a set designer who lives in New York with her playwright husband, was visiting Wyoming and she also shared with us:

"When I first got sober, I was too foggy to really see that I was sober! I just continued the old behavior. As my head cleared up, I *saw* life! That's when I started feeling guilty and embarrassed about sober sex.

"When I was still drinking, I lived with my drinking alcoholic husband for fifteen years. The whole sexual thing was extremely bizarre: it involved degrading sex in which he would hurt me. We would set the stage for such activity by talking a lot about really sick situations, like being two years old. When I got sober, I couldn't do those things.

"I not only didn't want to say those things — I didn't want anyone to *hear* me say those things! When I was drinking, though, I never gave that a thought!

"I *missed* it; but I couldn't *do* it, sober. That was a real adjustment. And I got kind of depressed over it for a while. That whole adjustment made sober sex a letdown, for a while. You *can* do it sober, but you feel a little ridiculous!

"Drunk, I would sing. I would play scenes from movies! I thought I was wonderful! I would go see a Julie Christie movie, and I would come home, and I would be Julie Christie in bed! I'd pout; I'd think I was a size-2 dress, I'd toss my hair; I would look very British, thoughtful and *so* uncaring about whether he'd stay or not. I would feel like a wonderful movie star, for about an hour and a half.

"Sometimes I can recapture the fun, sober; that wonderful ability to make believe, in bed. But only because my husband is sober and turned out to be very agile about that, himself. He loses himself in bed, in fantasy. And he doesn't watch me to see how I'm too clumsy, or whatever. And that freed me up. Now we're *into* a 'poetry' minus the sick games, minus the hurt, minus the cruelty."

There was a long silence. I think a lot of the people in the group were afraid to share their experiences after hearing Sheila. They were comparing themselves to her. Feeling inadequate. Feeling that she not only had sex with her husband now, as many of them were not doing, but she was enjoying it, and living life fully. No fears. No humdrum-ness either. A cosmopolitan life! They were absolutely forgetting that Sheila, too, has her areas of life that are very vulnerable. Like we all do.

Finally, Karen burst in with her story:

"Well, my situation's different! It's not so hot! I live with an active drunk, and so we have that fantasy life! It's the *only* good thing about our relationship.

"But, overall, since *I've* been sober, sex has become so much less important than it was. I would never admit it, drunk, because I thought I was 'socially conscious,' but I was so vulnerable to the world and its pain. So, sex was all important as a trade-off. At one time, I would have hotly denied that. But I knew that if I didn't sleep with my husband, he would not stay around. *I had nothing else to give.* I was spent, emotionally. I needed to be taken care of. I could not give — although I *believed* the illusion that I was a caretaker."

Bob told us, "All my life, whenever I had sex, I had a drink or two or four or ten! Sober, I had nothing to give me courage or to make me more amorous or to hide behind. Or to make me feel more virile.

"I was also more afraid of being rejected when I was sober. Drunk, I could ignore those thoughts. *Everything is more immediate when you are drunk.* I was incapable of thinking through the future and reasonably thinking about this person rejecting me. After a few drinks, I was only sensation; I was totally in the present; and I could see only the segmented person in front of me. Maybe about one one-thousandth of my today's perception was at work, then. My vision was impaired. My hearing, my smell, my touch, my cells were all impaired. *It was like 99 percent of me was shut down entirely and the other one percent was going 500 percent in an erroneous direction.* I was high-charged, but not really connecting. At the same time, however, I was under the misconception that I *was* highly connecting.

"So when I got sober, I was scared to death. On a daily, weekly basis, I became painfully more aware of myself and the world. It was hard enough to incorporate all this newness and anxiety about it; then to channel myself in an intimate, the most intimate way, with another?! I could barely connect with *me*!

"I finally got the courage to get involved when I realized that I could stay in love with just myself for just so long!" he laughed.

*   *   *   *   *   *

What about Kevin, the British-looking executive whose very attractive wife has been sober twenty years and with whom he has never been able to have sex— since she sobered up?

And then there's Diane, whose husband can't have a sexual relationship with *her*, now that he's sober. What about her?

If Kevin were not so tall, he would appear slight. His thinness is so narrow, he looks like a Giacometti sculpture. He is a quiet person. He tells me that his colleagues suspect that his low profile around the office must mean that he stops holding it all in at home. That he must be a roaring typhoon there.

"Huh," he shrugged. "I don't even bring up what bothers me. I guess I pride myself on the amiability of our relationship. But we never have sex. And we don't argue about it. And we don't look for it outside our relationship. I guess that with AIDS today, fewer people than ever do that. But I just don't want to be with her when she's stone-sober."

It took several weeks of talking with Kevin, about alcoholic relationships in general, before he would talk further about this.

"My colleagues certainly think my wife is very attractive. As *I* do. And I have moments when I am very turned on by her. But, I just can't face her, sober. Not sexually. She was so different when she was drinking. Don't get me wrong. I certainly am delighted that she's sober. We have a great relationship! But, she's not the ephemeral, slip-of-a-woman she was when she drank. She had *abandon* then. She was so 'airy' that she seemed so approachable. Now, she's so 'there,' she's scary. She's so strong, so *person*, now."

Kevin, once he expressed himself for the very first time in his life about this issue, allowed himself to see a therapist to explore whether he could salvage this aspect of his marital relationship. To his surprise, when he became strong enough to tell his wife he was seeing a therapist, and wanted her to talk to the therapist, too, she gladly consented and went. The silence was broken. He was very surprised to see that his wife understood perfectly well how he felt. She missed that part in herself, too! She had been afraid to express it just like Kevin had been. Likewise, she was embarrassed about it. Before long, they were able to try to 'start over,' in a sense. This time, they were both shy, but able to be protective of each other, and they gently eased into a sexual relationship.

Diane and her husband, Tim, had a tougher time working things out. I met with Tim privately, as they both requested. Tim poured out his feelings after a long struggle that involved pain and embarrassment and shame. "I think I feel Diane is 'too familiar.' I was used to being only a minute or two in a chance encounter. I was so painfully shy that I couldn't see those women again. I see her day after day. I feel like a teenager! I think I'm really shy!

"When I was drunk, I never hung around long enough to see anyone's defects of character. But I do *see* hers, and I don't *like* them! I translate it into 'I don't like *her.*' I know I'm sounding so young. I feel young. Not good-young. Childish."

Diane said, "I figured it was something like that. But I can't help feeling rejected." She was quiet for a while. "But I guess it's not *me*. He'd feel that way with anyone since he's sober. He just is turned off to *reality*."

They worked out a plan:

(1). They would do more mundane things apart, and not be on top of each other all the time, so the 'mystery' would reenter their relationship.

(2). They would do more *fun* things together, so they would gradually get the spark back in their relationship.

(3). They would not use each other so much as emotional sounding boards; they'd get the help they needed from others for a while; and they would allow the old wounds to heal.

(4). They would try to make no self-judgments; they would both try very hard to remain wondrous and divorced from results.

It's not what they would like it to be, three months later, but they are both more involved with each other than they were for years. They touch each other, they are compassionate, they kid each other. And they flirt with each other.

They are beginning to be delighted that they find themselves living in the same house!

The workbook section that follows each chapter is intended not only to heighten self-awareness, but it assumes that all of us, at some times, are reluctant to change because of our fears. Each workbook section leads us to examine those fears, and find ways to diminish their intensity, lessen their impact, and get in touch with that inner-permission-source that will allow us to take very small steps toward healing that are less fear-making than the giant steps we may have thought we had to take. And in instances when you are immobilized by terror — where you feel there are no viable options — I hope you can find it in yourself to allow yourself to "put the information on the shelf," so you can retrieve it later. All of us have those times and fears. The lucky ones are able to admit to it.

Write your feelings and thoughts on the following four comments, concerning the chapter you just read:

1.)   I feel both relieved and frightened that this subject is spoken about so frankly in this chapter.

2.)   My problem is finding someone I feel comfortable enough with to be able to talk about this subject.

3.)   I like the way Max says, "It's just another thing in life." That somewhat calms my fears about even contemplating dealing with this subject. I tend to dramatize.

4.)   I never thought about the fact that when I was drinking, I wasn't really 'connecting' with people or situations. I thought I was.

Quickly draw two circles on this page, one of them representing you, and one representing your spouse.

Now, without giving any "thought" to your answers, write in one word or two, in each of the circles, describing: your feelings toward your spouse, concerning your sexual relationship; and his or hers toward you (what you think those feelings are).

Write the phrases that you could "hear" your parent (s) say, if he or she were responding to this chapter: _____

_____

_____

_____

How do these phrases of your parent (s) still evoke reactions in you today? _____

_____

_____

_____

If your spouse, boyfriend, girlfriend, etc., were to read this chapter, given the history of your relationship, what do you believe would be his or her response? _____

_____

How do you feel about that probable response? _____

_____

Do you think you would encounter uncomfortable feelings if you would share your innermost thoughts and feelings about this chapter with your closest loved one?

_____

_____

_____

Do you feel there is any way to begin open communication with your closest loved one about the feelings you just expressed? Is there a way to begin discussion about your feelings honestly, without making yourself too vulnerable? (and in a way in which that person could really *hear* you?) _____

_____

_____

_____

_____

_____

_____

_____

What subjects come to your mind as you read this chapter? What subjects do you believe are necessary to deal with, at some time (today or in the future), to continue your own healing?

_____

_____

_____

_____

_____

_____

After reading this chapter, what area of difficulty arises in your mind—an area that brings up emotional pain, when you try to change your attitude toward it, or change your life-style concerning that area? _____

_____

_____

_____

_____

_____

_____

How can you lessen the pain that you anticipated in the above question? Can you do so by lowering your expectations of yourself? Can you anticipate taking a beginning *very* small step to change, instead of big ones? Can you allow yourself times of rest, of break, between changes? Do you have a spiritual program of recovery that buffers the pain surrounding this issue?_____

_____

_____

_____

_____

_____

Belief systems can either increase or decrease psychic pain. What are your intrinsic beliefs about the ideas presented in this chapter? Do they dovetail with what you were taught as a child? Are they ideas that protected you as a child, but that hinder your growth as an ethical adult? _____

_____

_____

_____

_____

_____

_____

What are your beliefs about the higher power? Do you think that God is basically a punishing God? If you felt fear when dealing with the questions at the end of this chapter, does this at all have to do with a concept of a punishing God? _____

_____

_____

_____

_____

_____

_____

List positive change (s) you have already made in your life, concerning the issue (s) in this chapter and how they have affected you. _____

_____

_____

_____

_____

_____

Describe the details — the actual emotional steps —of your journey to reach this more comfortable state that you talked about in the previous question. _____

_____

_____

_____

_____

_____

How may you learn from this journey, to face other situations in life that seem difficult, but that are opportunities for growth? _____

_____

_____

_____

Have you had any losses, any setbacks, around any of the issues in this chapter? Have you had times when you felt you were "going backwards," not growing, even though you were trying to get through a difficult situation? Were there times when you felt like staying in a sick situation, and not trying to grow at all? When you liked it the way it was?_____

_____

_____

_____

_____

_____

Having come through this, and faced it somehow, do you see growth, perhaps despite yourself? _____

_____

_____

_____

_____

_____

_____

Sex and "Games" and Recovery

"If any of you lacks wisdom, he should ask God, who gives generously to all without finding fault, and it will be given to him." (James 1:5).

2

The most difficult thing Jeanne has to deal with today in her marriage to a sober alcoholic is the guilt that surrounds her dissatisfaction that her spouse is still 'playing games.'

Jeanne feels, as do most of her other friends in her small-town-Iowa, family-recovery group, that she should be 'grateful' for his sobriety in a totally nonquestioning way. Like an obedient child, she should not 'talk back,' should not question what he does, should not consider 'running away' from a situation which half her group would give their eyeteeth for: he's finally conscious all day.

I find that spouses of alcoholics who are themselves

ACOAs (Adult Children of Alcoholics), incorporate these myths into their very bone marrow in ways that non-ACOA spouses of alcoholics do not even comprehend.

If a spouse is still 'playing at' being sexual with others or is overtly sexual, and is obviously not wanting to change that behavior — indeed, defends it vigorously —or just flat denies it (thereby providing a fertile, crazy-making situation in the home) — most non-ACOA spouses would go through pain, to be sure...*but they would probably not doubt their sanity, not doubt their perception, and not doubt that they had the inherent right to leave — at least not to the bizarre extent that adult children of alcoholics who are spouses of alcoholics do.*

Both groups (spouses who *are* ACOAs and those who *are not* ACOAs), due to living with alcoholism in marriage, tend to lose self-confidence and temporarily lose the ability to conceive of themselves as being able to live alone without terror. Therefore, both groups tend to stay even in violent situations. However, when you add the overlay of self-doubt, feelings of 'insanity,' and such extreme loyalty (that belongs only to the realm of God) that ACOAs give to their alcoholic spouses — you have a situation where, without treatment (in Al-Anon and/or family counseling) that understands alcoholic families, the spouse usually stays and stays with alcoholism. She often does not leave until she is either treated for suicidal depression, or physical disease may take over, or other psychiatric disorders can manifest.

Jeanne, not trusting herself, doesn't even believe she has the right to 'see' what is going on unless others see it, too. So she constantly tells her friends what is happening, and half of them don't believe her. Her spouse is an 'upright' member of the community, and is house-devil/street-angel.

She doesn't *really* hear those who tell her she is not crazy; she "hears" them, but cannot move from her situation for fear that *just possibly* there is a grain of truth in the words of those who say she is 'overreacting.'

Until the whole world gives her permission, Jeanne feels she cannot leave him.

And even if they do, she is too scared to do so.

Sally and George are in a group of recovered alcoholics and their spouses, at their local hospital that has an outpatient center for sober people and their families who want to work on marital problems, children problems, and their own spiritual growth.

Sally and George are getting close to three of the other four couples. Actually, George is friendly with everyone in the group. Sally is 'colder' to Karen, the sober-alcoholic wife of Ken. (Sally and Ken are the fourth couple in that group.)

George seems 'easygoing, friendly, twinkling'; Sally seems reserved, cold-ish, 'uptight,' wary, and sarcastic.

Why?

Nothing came out about this from the members of the group. They all expressed surprise and embarrassment and bafflement when the group leaders brought it up. Why were the "auras" of Sally and George as different as night and day?

Fortunately, the counselors also talked with each person alone on a regular basis. And the head counselor was very, very much in tune to these alcoholic family 'games' that seem to become manifest so often.

"Sally, do you think George has a bit of a 'philandering eye?'" she asked.

Sally, uncomfortable, was unwilling to get herself into another crazy-making venture. Her husband had told her often enough that she overreacts. She wasn't going to get the official therapy stamp of approval on *that* diagnosis! So, she felt her way carefully, hoping there was not a trap.

"Maybe. Do you?"

The counselor knew why she hedged. She *felt* her fear.

"Yes. And I believe you are too scared to say it. Does he invalidate your perception? Are you too frightened to talk about it? Do you just get a knot in your stomach?"

Sally burst into tears and explained that this was their story for their entire seven-year marriage. And it had not changed since sobriety. Oh, yes, she was happy he worked and came home and they had a family life, but she hated this group. Coming to it sickened her, because George and Karen flirted with each other.

"I see that, Sally," the counselor said. "Karen's husband seems to respond to that behavior by just getting depressed. I *see* your anger. Karen's husband is not even in touch with his, yet."

Of course, getting validated was just the first step for Sally. She had to be led through all her fears, expressing them and then gently dealing with them, to help her to get ready to do what was really best for her, should her husband not want to change.

And this situation was fortunate. George was more willing to keep his marriage than the very-young behavior of flirting with everyone. He also realized he had some serious problems with his self-image. That his flirting was, to a large extent, his trying to get validated that he was an attractive man. He was not at all aware, before he was confronted with this behavior, that he was so insecure about his physical attractiveness.

He was also encouraged to seek other role models. He found sponsors in A.A. who were men who felt good about themselves and did not need to act in this manner.

He observed them and found in them that they exuded a degree of self-confidence he envied. He wanted what they had.

He looked back at his former role models. From his heightened level of self-esteem, he was rather shocked to see that the people who acted like he used to act seemed desperate, sad. The look in their eyes was not really 'seeing' others (as he thought his flirting had been), but a desperate looking for mirrors in others' eyes — seeking a bottomless need for self-approval.

Looking back, Sally and George realized they both had come from alcoholic families and had manifested their own sicknesses — their fears — in different ways.

In the A.A. and Al-Anon programs of recovery, it is said that one needs to:

— make amends for injuries done to others, except when to do so would injure them.

— become cognizant of the "spiritual axiom," which states that 'whenever I am troubled, the trouble lies within.'

Now, at first glance, these two may seem mutually exclusive —contradictory. If you are responsible for the feelings of others, and need to make amends — where do you fit in the idea that 'no one can keep anyone troubled'?

The two ideas are *both* valid. No one is a robot. All of us have feelings. Therefore, we *can* injure others. Hence, amends are necessary.

Also true, though, is that you are *ultimately* responsible for your feelings. This does *not* absolve others from amends to you, nor does it diminish your pain. However, *they* are not going to be around all the time, re-feeling your pain. You are, if you choose to. ('Resent' means to 're-feel'.) Until you can *detach* from your pain, you're *attached* to it. No matter who caused it. No matter if you set yourself up for it. No matter if it was accidental. This spiritual axiom that tells you that if you are troubled, the trouble lies within, tells you that no one is absolved, but that you have great hope that you do not have to be a slave to continually hurt as a result of someone else's behavior. You have tools to free yourself. In fact, you have 'spiritual permission' to stop hurting.

Write your feelings and thoughts on the following four comments, concerning the chapter you just read:

1.)   I know my alcoholic wife is trying to play with my head. I go from holding it in and not saying anything, to finally accusing her. But nothing changes.

2.)   I'm an ACOA. I don't think I have the right to leave a relationship until I can get everyone I know to agree that my spouse is hurting me.

3.)   I've been to three counselors and two ministers. They didn't really *see* the alcoholic games. Not at all.

4.)   I never wanted to agree that we're all ultimately responsible for our own feelings. I thought that that let my alcoholic wife off the hook when she hurt me. You know: "That's *your* problem, your feelings," she would say, as she hurt me.

On the top half this page, draw a circle representing you, draw one representing your spouse, and draw a circle representing an attractive member of the opposite sex. Draw these circles with either light lines, strong and heavy lines, sensual lines, "angry" lines, or however you wish. Place names in the circles for identification.

On the bottom half of this page, draw a circle representing your feelings about what you drew on the top half of this page, after looking at it for a few minutes.

Is this circle timid? Angry? In motion? Bottled up? Able to move? Thoughtful?

Write the phrases that you could "hear" your parent (s) say, if he or she were responding to this chapter: _____

_____

_____

_____

How do these phrases of your parent (s) still evoke reactions in you today? _____

_____

_____

_____

If your spouse, boyfriend, girlfriend, etc., were to read this chapter, given the history of your relationship, what do you believe would be his or her response? _____

_____

How do you feel about that probable response? _____

_____

Do you think you would encounter uncomfortable feelings if you would share your innermost thoughts and feelings about this chapter with your closest loved one?

_____

_____

_____

Do you feel there is any way to begin open communication with your closest loved one about the feelings you just expressed? Is there a way to begin discussion about your feelings honestly, without making yourself too vulnerable? (and in a way in which that person could really *hear* you?) _____

_____

_____

_____

_____

_____

_____

What subjects come to your mind as you read this chapter? What subjects do you believe are necessary to deal with, at some time (today or in the future), to continue your own healing?

_____

_____

_____

_____

_____

_____

After reading this chapter, what area of difficulty arises in your mind—an area that brings up emotional pain, when you try to change your attitude toward it, or change your life-style concerning that area? _____

_____

_____

_____

_____

_____

_____

_____

How can you lessen the pain that you anticipated in the above question? Can you do so by lowering your expectations of yourself? Can you anticipate taking a beginning *very* small step to change, instead of big ones? Can you allow yourself times of rest, of break, between changes? Do you have a spiritual program of recovery that buffers the pain surrounding this issue?_____

_____

_____

_____

_____

_____

_____

Belief systems can either increase or decrease psychic pain. What are your intrinsic beliefs about the ideas presented in this chapter? Do they dovetail with what you were taught as a child? Are they ideas that protected you as a child, but that hinder your growth as an ethical adult? _____

_____

_____

_____

_____

_____

_____

What are your beliefs about the higher power? Do you think that God is basically a punishing God? If you felt fear when dealing with the questions at the end of this chapter, does this at all have to do with a concept of a punishing God? _____

_____

_____

_____

_____

_____

_____

List positive change (s) you have already made in your life, concerning the issue (s) in this chapter and how they have affected you. _____

_____

_____

_____

_____

_____

Describe the details — the actual emotional steps —of your journey to reach this more comfortable state that you talked about in the previous question. _____

_____

_____

_____

_____

_____

How may you learn from this journey, to face other situations in life that seem difficult, but that are opportunities for growth? _____

_____

_____

_____

Have you had any losses, any setbacks, around any of the issues in this chapter? Have you had times when you felt you were "going backwards," not growing, even though you were trying to get through a difficult situation? Were there times when you felt like staying in a sick situation, and not trying to grow at all? When you liked it the way it was?_____

_____

_____

_____

_____

_____

Having come through this, and faced it somehow, do you see growth, perhaps despite yourself? _____

_____

_____

_____

_____

_____

_____

Adult Children
of Alcoholics:
Guilt, Shame, Abuse
and Isolation

"My soul finds rest in God alone; my salvation comes from Him. He alone is my rock and my salvation, He is my fortress, I will never be shaken: (Ps. 62:1,2).

3

"My mother would put me in the tub. She would insist on it. Even when I got older. She would be brusque, and then she would throw a washcloth at me. Her face would get white, she would get pink spots on her cheeks, and she would stare at me. Finally, when I couldn't take it any more, I screamed at her to get out. She never came into the bathroom, any more." (The narrator is Chris, age fifty-three; his mother was an alcoholic who is now deceased.)

"No one mentioned sex. When I started dating, my mother just said, 'Don't!' Back when I was a young teenager, and I babysat, a drunk grandfather brought me home (they were raising the children), and he'd let go of the steering wheel and giggle when I'd grab it so we wouldn't have an accident, and then he would put his hands on me. I finally told my mother. She got very angry and told me it wasn't true, that he 'was from...family, a very good family in town.' My mother took pills; tranquilizers."

(The narrator is Cyndie, her mother and father were alcoholics; both are now dead.)

Katya shared her story also: "I used to 'get into' light abuse, like spanking. I feel embarrassed about saying that now. And we 'got into' costumes. Well, we didn't have any money for good costumes! Ours were pretty raggedy," [We both laughed.] "And one day, my husband wanted to buy a surgeon's table! Do you know how sick I was? The only real reason I didn't want to, was because it didn't go with the decor! And I was also worried that visitors might ask what it was for! I thought I couldn't tell my A.A. sponsor about *that*! But, maybe I could; she's a nurse!"

Obviously, what we needed in this interview was a little bit of humor to break the ice caused by her nervousness. Each of the people I was sitting with had shared their experiences in ACOA (Adult Children of Alcoholics) meetings; but none had shared so deeply about their sexual and sensual feelings and experiences that they had always kept hidden from others — because of shame.

Shame, guilt, isolation — all to bizarre degrees — and rationalizations to keep them secret and to pretend that the feelings-on-top-of-the-feelings were the real ones.

"Not that I believe that we ACOAs have the corner on shame and guilt — but I do think we have it to greater extremes and for longer durations, and with more intensity, than do adults from functional homes." This was Katya's sister talking: the oldest of five children; blonde; medium height; about thirty-five pounds overweight; fifty-seven years old. Katya was as thin as her sister was heavy; she was very tall with dark hair and blue eyes. Katya was the youngest.

TOBY: "Do you have the gut feeling, like I do, that most women today who get into embarrassing and humiliating and abusive situations with men, are adult children of alcoholics? I think that the women who lose the most self-esteem are ACOAs. Many other kids had *some* dose of self-esteem as they were growing up. They had it to start with."

KATYA: "I'm a recovering alcoholic as well as a recovering adult child of alcoholics. And in terms of sex, the only kind of sex I experienced as a young woman (before marriage and before sobriety) was with a mentor I had, on the job.

He wanted me to hurt him, physically. And I got into that with him quite willingly.

"I'm only now beginning to face what that means about myself. About the anger I suppressed since my infancy. I grew up with an alcoholic father whom I hated. This man — this mentor — I had complete contempt for, when I thought about him personally. When I looked at him only professionally, I had respect for him and liked him. But when I thought about him as a *man* — it was like something deep and dark and so angry happened inside of me.

"Since that 'relationship,' I've had the opposite experience. When I got sober and some of my anger melted, I found my husband, and now he and I are in a mirror-opposite of that prior experience. *He* abuses *me*. It seems that under the anger that made me feel so powerful, was a little girl who was frightened to death and needs to be punished for having been so angry —and for having some of that anger still there. And I say 'needs to be punished' because he doesn't make me do this.

"I am a willing participant. I can only believe that I sort of like this because I am not yet healed from my childhood.

"I've never said this stuff before, and I didn't even know that I felt it. Or thought it."

We were all very quiet for a while.

TOBY: "Were you in therapy during this time?"

KATYA: "Yes."

TOBY: "Did it occur to you to say anything to the therapist?"

KATYA: "It occurred to me that this was not okay with me even thought it might be a valuable piece of information to tell a therapist. I was not able to; you're the only person I have ever told. This is the first time I have told anyone."

CYNDIE:"When I was in therapy (somewhere between fifteen and twenty years before I got to A.A.), I remember I used to alternate between despairing time in therapy and feeling like I had to entertain my therapist. I wanted to be the best, the funniest, wittiest, brightest patient the therapist ever had. And I considered myself a raconteur.

"I just sort of went through story after story that was wild. The ones that were not too humiliating. But if it was too humiliating and too disgusting without a redeeming, witty factor, I left it out. But, I was so ashamed of it. And, I'm thinking about me as an ACOA and other people I've talked to who are ACOAs, that we get ourselves into more self-shaming things than do other people who admitted they were alcoholics — but who did not grow up in alcoholic families. Even if they were drinking at the time, they didn't seem to get into such scummy, humiliating things. The sense of *shame* — I didn't even realize the *depth* of shame I had when I got sober. I remember hearing people talking about shame. And, I said 'shame?' It seemed totally irrelevant to me."

KATYA: "I don't *think* I ever did anything because of fear I would be abandoned, but that might have entered into it. Maybe that *was* part of it. Every time I saw this man I felt totally humiliated. Yet, there was something I wasn't willing to give up. I mean I could have told him to go fly a kite any time, but that relationship lasted until ten years ago. That's how long it went on. Eleven years! That's a long time. Oddly enough, he contacted me maybe two years ago and I saw him. I don't even know why. He did ask a favor of me at that time which was interesting. He asked if I would go to a bar to find him a woman who would beat him. He knew that *I* was no longer willing to play that game. That had become clear. I had had my first experience of knowing that God was trying to get in touch with me. I would get to where I hated myself so much that I would say, 'You cannot do this any more, no matter what. You cannot!' But I always did it again.

"After I met a Christian woman who helped me, the next time he called me, I was able to say (and it's one of the truly amazing things that occurred), I was able to say I had learned something about Jesus, and something about calling on the protection of Jesus.

"When he called I said, 'I won't be able to see you. You see, I've turned my life over to Jesus and I can't do that any more.' He did such a quick turnaround! He didn't want to say another word to me! He heard the word 'Jesus' and it terrified him and he went away! I had thought many times that this man was satanic. It seems to be such a corny word — but that's the way I felt about him. He was devil-driven or at the very least, related to the darkest forces. Sure enough, I called on Jesus and this man couldn't end our conversation soon enough. That was the last time I heard from him until about two years ago, when he wanted me to find this woman. He told me he had been looking all those years for someone to take my place. What a 'precious relationship' I had been for him — how important, and so on. He's now dead, which is interesting. He died maybe a year or so ago. He was young. He might have been forty by then. My girl friend said, 'Oh, did you know that so-and-so died?' She thought I might be interested because she had no idea about what kind of relationship we had had. She knew we saw each other occasionally. She didn't think it was sexual at all. She knows I am happily married now. That's all."

CYNDIE:"I used to jump into relationships. I would meet somebody at a party, sit up all night and talk, and think that this was "it" and move in with him, all within twelve hours. And I would do this repeatedly. It was because I was so desperate. People say, 'Oh, I was desperate,' but what they mean is that they went to bed on a first date. I'm talking about *moving in* within twelve hours, and then realizing that it's so crazy that you run out screaming like a maniac after a couple of weeks. You run out into the street and grab just any old place to live in. You don't even do intelligent apartment shopping, because you need a place to sleep. You 'crash' in girlfriends' houses. And, then, you go through periods of abstinence to protect yourself, and then, you become so desperately lonely you go to a party and meet somebody and you sit up all night, have one of those 'soul sessions,' and move in within ten hours. This time you think, 'This is it.' This is the wonderful, wonderful person who is going to save me, and I'll never be lonely again and he'll be wonderful.' "

As I listened to these women talk, I saw how they ran the gamut: some of them were the prototype of a fearful woman — others were the typical Strong Woman. All were adult children of alcoholics. All had been in therapy for many years. All of them had made *very tiny* inroads into 'answers' for their problems in therapy. All of them felt that something was intrinsically wrong with them. None of them knew (before very recently) that they had been acting in typical 'cookie-cutter' fashion — they were duplicates of each other — in terms of the *bizarre* degree to which they acted in self-deprecating ways with men. All of them found that in the therapy groups they were in, the clients who were *not* adult children of alcoholics (ACOAs) had the same problems as those who *were* ACOAs — but to 'normal' degrees. All the ACOAs had these problems to degrees that baffled their therapists.

"You are so bright! *Why* can't you let go of this degrading relationship?!" the therapists would cry. Everyone else in the groups who came from non-alcoholic homes were able to extricate themselves and *keep* themselves extricated from these abusive relationships after about a year or so of therapy.

After three years of therapy, the ACOAs were beginning to detach a *very little bit* from abuse, but only a little. All of them felt they could not measure up to the others in their therapy groups. They felt like failures in 'Self-Esteem 101.'

This was true of most of the ACOA women I spoke with, and most of the men....

Chuck is an engineer in a large midwestern city. He lives with his wife and four children. His mother, who lived near them, passed away over ten years ago. His alcoholic father died when he was very young.

Chuck is four years sober, now, and he is just beginning to get out of this intense emotional pain he's been experiencing all his life.

Chuck's an avid tennis player, and we met for this interview at the athletic club, over sandwiches and carrot juice.

TOBY: "What does 'shame' mean to you?"

CHUCK:"Shame is guilt, but it's guilt that *everybody knows*! It's when I feel real guilty about something and I'm sure everyone around knows what's going on with me."

TOBY: "Then there is an added element of exposure and humiliation."

CHUCK:"Yes. That's exactly right. In addition, it carries an element of, 'I'm guilty about this, and I'm all bad.' or 'I'm no good.'"

TOBY: "Your father was an alcoholic."

CHUCK:"Yes. There are a couple of pieces of evidence to support this. One is my own alcoholism, which began very early and became manifest almost immediately when I took my first drink. The second is that I identify so strongly with the adult children's movement. I was in a family treatment center and was processing some other things, but one day my counselor came to me and showed me one of those adult children's 'laundry lists.' I immediately knew that was *me*.

"I was isolated while growing up, not only from my parents, but also from my peers. The only chum I can ever remember having was a playmate, a little girl."

TOBY: "How old were you?"

CHUCK:"Five or six. One of the surprising things is that though I remember very little, I remember the girl's name. I don't much remember what she looked like, but I remember that her name was Brenda. I remember what we did. We played cops and robbers on our tricycles. That was my only playmate. Ever.

"There was a clear-cut message from my mother, (and maybe from my father) that I was spending too much time with Brenda."

TOBY: "How were you supposed to spend your time?"

CHUCK:"I have no idea, but I know I spent the remainder of it glued to the radio. Being very shy and alone and not having either male or female companions, my relationships with girls were totally a fantasy world. The upshot of that was that I became super-shy around women."

TOBY: "You told me earlier you were chronically depressed. Did that bring on a kind of inertia about changing anything in your life?"

CHUCK:"You betcha it did. Inertia. I was frequently brought to the attention of the headmaster in school as an underachiever. I scored very high on those stupid tests, and people wondered why I didn't *shine*.

"And I sensed that people had never been very important in my life. I used to think I was too lazy to call people, and reach out to people. But, largely I believe it was not important to me. Other people had *never* been important, because I grew up so isolated.

"Once, when on vacation (I was six), a little girl turned to her mother right after lunch and said (about me), 'Wasn't he rude at lunch?' and I had no idea what she meant, but I sure know what my feelings were at the time: 'Girl, I don't *need* you!' and I remember thinking about all the other kids around and I said, 'Babes, I don't need *you*, either!'

"I remember when I *first* felt lonely: I was already an adult! If you ever read *I Never Promised You a Rose Garden* or saw the movie, you might remember that it was about this little girl who liked to burn herself with cigarettes. She was so sick she could not feel it. And, one of the most poignant scenes for me was, as she was getting well, she sneaked into the bathroom and lit a cigarette and burned her arm. Her face lit up and she said, 'It hurts, it hurts!' And, that was what I was thinking of when I could first *feel* the loneliness. That's the first time I ever remember identifying a lonely feeling. I was forty years old."

That little girl in the book that Chuck identifies with was 'psychotic.' Yet, tens of millions of adult children of alcoholics — people who are achievers, highly functioning, not at all labeled as psychotic —are living on the edge, not feeling, or feeling to bizarre degrees. Again, these people often 'got into therapy,' only to often find themselves feeling even more on the fringe, since the therapists often cannot relate to the degree of detachment or attachment that ACOAs manifest.

We need to remember that ACOAs are not freaks that seem to have fatal flaws that sprang from nowhere. That we are not 'typically neurotic' or 'borderline' or somehow mutant in our severe alienation. There is a perfectly sound reason for our deep craters of need. And when we can begin to see the *logic* of our development and realize that we need not fear that we cannot ever 'get well,' we begin to heal quickly. We begin to lose our fear of looking at, facing, our pasts.

We see that squarely looking at our alcoholic childhoods is the first step in our salvation, and not a thing that will get in the way of our 'getting on with life.'

If we do not face the past at *some* point in our adult lives, it will become harder and harder to 'get on with life,' because our childhoods in alcoholism will cause us to stumble over the past — over and over and over. We need to lose our rationalizations that cover our fears about even *peeking* at our parent's alcoholism.

Write your feelings and thoughts on the following four comments, concerning the chapter you just read:

1.)   I still have a lot of secrets. I still feel an irrational shame about what my parents did to me, as a child. I am an ACOA.

2.)   I've never told anyone I was abused.

3.)   I've never wanted anyone to know just how desperate I've felt. I've said I was desperate, but I never told my most humiliating experiences.

4.)   I've put up with a lot of abuse, so I wouldn't be alone.

Draw circles at random, all over the page, representing yourself, your parents, your siblings. Name the circles.

Notice the placement of the circles. How close are you to your parents? How close are your brothers, sisters, to your parents? If you were an only child, how far in from the borders of the page did you allow yourself to go? What placement would you rather see, if you could re-do your childhood?

Write the phrases that you could "hear" your parent (s) say, if he or she were responding to this chapter: _____

_____

_____

_____

How do these phrases of your parent (s) still evoke reactions in you today? _____

_____

_____

_____

If your spouse, boyfriend, girlfriend, etc., were to read this chapter, given the history of your relationship, what do you believe would be his or her response? _____

_____

How do you feel about that probable response? _____

_____

Do you think you would encounter uncomfortable feelings if you would share your innermost thoughts and feelings about this chapter with your closest loved one?

_____

_____

_____

Do you feel there is any way to begin open communication with your closest loved one about the feelings you just expressed? Is there a way to begin discussion about your feelings honestly, without making yourself too vulnerable? (and in a way in which that person could really *hear* you?) _____

_____

_____

_____

_____

_____

_____

What subjects come to your mind as you read this chapter? What subjects do you believe are necessary to deal with, at some time (today or in the future), to continue your own healing?

_____

_____

_____

_____

_____

_____

After reading this chapter, what area of difficulty arises in your mind—an area that brings up emotional pain, when you try to change your attitude toward it, or change your life-style concerning that area? _____

_____

_____

_____

_____

_____

_____

_____

How can you lessen the pain that you anticipated in the above question? Can you do so by lowering your expectations of yourself? Can you anticipate taking a beginning *very* small step to change, instead of big ones? Can you allow yourself times of rest, of break, between changes? Do you have a spiritual program of recovery that buffers the pain surrounding this issue? _____

_____

_____

_____

_____

_____

_____

Belief systems can either increase or decrease psychic pain. What are your intrinsic beliefs about the ideas presented in this chapter? Do they dovetail with what you were taught as a child? Are they ideas that protected you as a child, but that hinder your growth as an ethical adult? _____

_____

_____

_____

_____

_____

_____

What are your beliefs about the higher power? Do you think that God is basically a punishing God? If you felt fear when dealing with the questions at the end of this chapter, does this at all have to do with a concept of a punishing God? _____

_____

_____

_____

_____

_____

_____

List positive change (s) you have already made in your life, concerning the issue (s) in this chapter and how they have affected you. _____

_____

_____

_____

_____

_____

Describe the details — the actual emotional steps —of your journey to reach this more comfortable state that you talked about in the previous question. _____

_____

_____

_____

_____

_____

How may you learn from this journey, to face other situations in life that seem difficult, but that are opportunities for growth? _____

_____

_____

_____

Have you had any losses, any setbacks, around any of the issues in this chapter? Have you had times when you felt you were "going backwards," not growing, even though you were trying to get through a difficult situation? Were there times when you felt like staying in a sick situation, and not trying to grow at all? When you liked it the way it was?_____

_____

_____

_____

_____

_____

_____

Having come through this, and faced it somehow, do you see growth, perhaps despite yourself? _____

_____

_____

_____

_____

_____

_____

_____

Adult Daughters of of Alcoholics and the Mistress Compulsion

"The Lord will keep you from all harm — He will watch over your life; The Lord will watch over your coming and going both now and forevermore" (Ps. 121:7,8).

4

Adult children of alcoholics have many compulsions, and obsessions. Near the top of the list, in order of self-destructiveness and destructiveness to others, is the mistress compulsion.

When 'she' is 'the other woman,' she is feared and hated.

When 'she' is our daughter, we agonize for her, we sometimes excuse her behavior, while screaming at her at other times. We try to find out 'why.'

When 'she' is us, we emphatically do *not* want to read how this is hurting us; we only want to know how to get 'him' to leave his wife.

That is, until we are hurting so much that we allow a *little* tiny bit of reality-light in.

And almost none of us *ever* connects this syndrome to our being from alcoholic families.

*   *   *   *

Kathleen was sitting in an A.A. meeting, listening to the speaker tell how he used to be a thief, when he was drinking, and how he tried to do the same kinds of things sober, but his conscience wouldn't let him. He had to return what he had taken. Kathleen whispered to the man who was sitting next to her,
"I used to steal husbands."

He answered, "They're hard to return!"

*   *   *   *

Kathleen was, in her own words, "embarrassingly typical" of the '60's woman, when she was still "out there" drinking. Sober five years, she recounted her 'other' life on the Lower East Side of Manhattan.

"My husband was a political cartoonist. He was involved in everything from the civil-rights movement to the Vietnam marches. I called him the movement's 'sketch-mascot.'"

She was uncomfortable about speaking of him. It was years since the divorce, and there hadn't been any children, but it was pushed down, *not out of*, her memory, and she didn't know how to exorcise it. "I knew he was having affairs...it was difficult in those days to be monogamous and still stay true to one's hip self-image. One had to 'politically justify' even your personal choices. At least, that's what I told myself."

Kathleen's apartment was large and yet intimate. A fine New York building, it housed mostly Europeanized intellectuals and writers whose backgrounds and tastes came together. Kathleen took me around to visit with some of her neighbors, to get a flavor of what she was like now: sober, and free of her old resentments that had led her to isolate herself from successful, mainstream people.

It was utterly charming to see her in this setting: burnished apartments; quiet, elegant friends. It was such a far cry from the days when she and her husband "proclaimed values that somehow linked the Radical Left with Buddhism."

I couldn't imagine this soft-spoken, straightforward, likable person, drunk or on pills. She was functioning well, now, and she was contented. She went on, "One simply did not decide to not have children because you wanted more time with your husband or to devote to your work. You said, instead, 'I don't want to add to the population growth.' Heaven forbid one should have said, "I don't want to share my money or my time." I think these were significant ways in which I began to lie to myself."

She sat quietly on the sofa. "My ex-husband had a lot of affairs. It ate me up inside. My terror, my depression, was so bad, I thought I'd die. But I couldn't leave, I was so scared to be alone. Later, when the pain of staying got worse than the pain of being alone, I left. I thought I was about to have a breakdown, and it was simply a matter that *that* was worse than being alone.

"Then, I started really drinking at bars, so I wouldn't feel alone. But, mostly, I drank, once I got there, to not notice where I was in the pecking order...to seem confident.

"I know, now, that I was married to an alcoholic. My father was one, too. When I look back, I always dated alcoholics or crazies. Nice men either terrified or bored me. I didn't know what to *do* with a nice man. It was so foreign, it terrified me. I just had to get away from them. I had to have a man in my life who had a 'fatal flaw.' *That* was familiar."

She went on. "I had a series of affairs, mostly with married men. I was afraid to take a chance and be 'the wife' and be rejected again. I had this false sense of glamour that *I* was 'the other woman.' I told myself, 'It's a trade-off.' I didn't know I was trading off my self-respect, my self-esteem. Those words seemed irrelevant, then.

I didn't know what they really meant, anyway. The poor self-image I started with went out the window entirely.

"I told myself more lies. That seems like such a strong word, doesn't it? But if I pretty-up what I did — what I still want to do, sometimes, now, even — I'll rationalize that I was basically acting as a victim, because of my childhood and my husband, instead of as the victimizer I really was. And I'd make sure I'd surround myself with sympathetic people, and I'd go to a therapist who'd be willing to excuse my behavior by helping me to divert into staying in the past. I'm not blaming therapists any more; I just know that I was a master con artist, and didn't even know it, most of the time.

"I thought I knew myself so well. I thought I was doing so well! I had wardrobes to match every environment I had to be in. I had the dresses to be with my staid parents; the prep clothes to meet certain men; the expensive-looking Bohemian ethnic dresses to impress the Villagers. Once, I was interviewing for a job at a publishing house, and I instinctively knew that they'd like the 30's British look although no one in 1963 was wearing that. So, I went to a thrift shop and bought a blue challis dress, real prim-looking. I bought pearls and short, white gloves from the five-and-dime, and put my hair in a bun. The interviewer said, 'I don't know why I'm hiring you on the spot...I never do that! There's something about you I like.' I didn't know when to stop being a chameleon, and not deceive *myself*.

"I believe there are so many of us out there: women whose fathers were alcoholics, who are looking for the father they never had in married men. And growing up in an alcoholic home makes you fantasize, want a glamorous, perfect world; expect it; and, yet, expect rottenness too.

"So, I went after this bundle of contradictions. And nothing has it so well in one package as an alcoholic married man...he's charming, unattainable, makes you feel special, taken care of. But, when some of the patina wears off, you realize it was an illusion. That *you've* done the only taking-care-of; that he's incapable of it. But if you 'love' him, you tell yourself excuses for him, like you did for your father. I started to realize it's a disease, but I wasn't well enough to differentiate between responsibility and disease.

"He's your vulnerable little boy, at times, and that's what hooks your guilt. To take care of him, cover for him.

"I told myself, 'he can't help it'...which made us both helpless.

"It is confusing, though, when I see him — them — hold down the most fantastic jobs. They *are* brilliant, you know.

"Was I different when I got sober? Well, take the rum out of the fruitcake, and you've still got a fruitcake — for a while at least.

"I had an easy first year of sobriety, as far as not having much pain from withdrawal from alcohol is concerned. This meant that instead of concentrating on the usual pain of early recovery, I was 'free' to concentrate on married men. And that's so unfortunate, because I thought I was weller than I was. If I hadn't been helped through the first year by my sponsor, I might have died. She helped me to say no to my disease and my compulsion around married men.

"That first year, I still had the old instincts. I didn't know *who* I was. I identified with Al-Anon spouses whose mates were womanizers. I shared their terror. And yet I was still attracted to married men. I was on 'both sides.' "

I had to postpone the next interview session with Kathleen. I realized I had terribly mixed feelings about her. Part of me liked the part of her that was non-threatening to other women, the part of her that identified as a 'wife.' And the other part of me didn't like her, and I knew that it masked a fear for women that got translated into anger. Not that I was a wonderful person, but my background didn't matter, just then, to me. I could have been Scarlett O'hara and I would have felt the same way: here was the 'kind of woman' who always threatened other women, whether these women identified with her behavior or not.

I told myself that she was the adult-child-of-an-alcoholic-victim, and that she could be anyone's daughter. That took only some of the anger away.

When we met again, I told her about this, and watched her. More than anything, her eyes and mouth told me there was no longer a sick, threatening woman there. Her mouth did not involuntarily smile as she recounted more horror stories. Her eyes just looked very sad. They didn't search mine, to look for vulnerability.

She had stopped romancing the past.

*   *   *   *

With time and distrust behind us, we got comfortable with each other, with our differences, and surprised each other to find ourselves so much alike. That's the trouble with interviews, I thought; they are so traumatic, requiring us to get so close, so soon. It's not fair to our nervous systems.

Kathleen said, "I was sober about three months when I was at a meeting for recovery and felt 'eyes' on me. I knew he'd been looking, before, but I didn't pay much attention. This time, he came up to me after the meeting, and he was so good-looking. He had that sober, yet beery, dissipated look I like, and told me he was a successful insurance agent who was unhappy because he couldn't spend all his time writing poetry. 'Just like Wallace Stevens!' he grinned down at me.

"That was all I needed to make me melt! I know it sounds '40's-movie corny, but that's what I did! I melted!

"They know how to hook me. Years ago, I stepped into a downtown 'hip' bar where all the newspapermen hang out all day, and this guy I'd never seen before said to me, "What a delightful little girl!" I melted then, too.

"Back to Steve. He was very, very married, and not about to not be. We didn't really talk...we just flirted from across the room at meetings and drove each other crazy. We'd 'wind up' at the same meetings, and 'signal' each other when people were talking. We'd circle each other after the meetings, talking to other people, but looking at each other. I used to do that in the seventh grade, with a boy who had a crush on me, and me on him, and even though he'd look at me, every day, from across the hall, I never had the nerve to talk with him. I thought he'd not respond because he was so cute and I wasn't one of the popular girls. One day, after lunch, when we were all outside, he pushed me to the ground, and sat on me, and shouted at me, "*Admit* you love me!" That was the happiest day of my junior-high life.

"Here we go again.

"I wanted to go to bed with Steve, but I couldn't. Not sober. I dreamed of going to his house. I dreamed his wife died — peacefully, of course. And we would have this clandestine affair until enough time passed — enough decent time, a year after the funeral.

"Other times, I'd fantasize that instead of getting married, I wouldn't marry him; I'd drive him crazy with wanting to own me. (That took care of any idea he'd have about getting tired of me if I were his 'wife'....he'd be kept at enough of a distance *forever* to keep him interested!)"

*　　　　*　　　　*　　　　*

We laughed a lot, but I felt a little awkward still. It was like eavesdropping and then being caught by someone who doesn't mind. Kathleen had gotten to the point of trusting me so much, and I began to realize how naive she really was.

She had so much guilt over her almost-childish fantasies; she didn't even know they were so "embarrassingly" young. They were the fantasies of a twelve-year-old — the same age she was when her father died.

*　　　　*　　　　*　　　　*

"Luckily for us, nothing happened. Absolutely nothing. I was living with my sponsor, and told her what was 'going on.' I thought I'd die from wanting him, but when, after meetings, he'd stand in front of his car, and look at me, as if to say 'get in ' — I couldn't. And I'd get depressed about my not being able to do what I'd done so easily before, when I was drinking. I was too scared. And I felt too guilty. I couldn't handle that kind of guilt. And, I knew the pain I was in for, when he would want out.

"I knew that *I* was the really vulnerable one. He was one with twenty-five years sobriety, and I was the one with three months.

"When I'd get really angry, depressed, and feel he had an advantage, vulnerability-wise, I consoled myself with the fact that *I* wasn't the married one, and could legitimately have a relationship or two or three some day, when I was well enough...and *he* was stuck in a marriage he couldn't really accept.

"But, then, I'd feel sorry for him, and my anger would go, and I'd be attracted to him all over again. Talk about a merry-go-round! And *all* between the ears!"

I asked her, "Did you ever try to stop?"

"Yeah. I prayed about it. But I was mad at God; I felt my Higher Power didn't want me to have any more fun in life. But I was too scared not to pray. One day, I was in agony, and someone I was talking with asked me, "Are you hurting enough to give up the edges of your pain?" That was the beginning of letting go. I thought I could just let go of the pain, and hold on to the rest, but it wasn't painful to let go of the rest. It just went, so slowly, easily, I didn't even know it was gone, until I started noticing I felt more peaceful. I'm glad I went through it. Now I don't have to go through it again, not so bad."

I told Kathleen that I had read that Bill Wilson, one of the co-founders of A.A., once said, "We've had more than our fair share of romance!" We both burst out laughing.

"So, did you go right from feeling like a seventh-grader to wellness? Obviously, it couldn't have been that easy, but you look so content," I asked Kathleen.

She answered, "A lot worked out, after being abstinent for two more years. I didn't realize that that fantasy world was connected to abstinence, escape. But, I shared what I was going through with other women, and I found out they were going through similar experiences, too.

"The baggage I brought in with me to A.A.! The old, violent, addictive dependence on men. That fear of being alone! I was told, 'no major changes the first year.' I didn't realize, then, that that wasn't only because the trauma of getting sober was enough. It was also because my brain would clear up enough for my perceptions to change. And who I'd be attracted to in a year, or two, or five, would be qualitatively different from whom I was interested in during those early months of sobriety."

"Why were you abstinent so long?" I asked.

"I was scared. I didn't think I could be burned again, like I was, by my husband — and stay sober."

"*Were* you burned again?" I asked.

"Yes, and no," she answered. "I waited two years. I started going into my old pattern of isolation, and then desperately running out into the first 'relationship' I found within two days. But sober, I *was* different. I held back, some. I didn't feel so desperate. I didn't move in with him in a week! I got involved when I knew I could survive it if he humiliated me.

"And he didn't. It just wasn't what either of us wanted. It was not fun, believe me, feeling disappointment because I wasn't what *he* wanted, either!

"It's a real trip to learn that we're all pretty much the same, and not the center of everyone else's universe. But, it's a lot better than feeling desperate and terror-stricken and driven all the time. I can even stay by myself at night, a lot, now. I never thought I was running from me." She added, "Those men...it's sad. None of us knew that they couldn't take care of me, emotionally. That they weren't supposed to."

There are fifteen million-plus adult daughters of alcoholics in the U.S. today. Sixty-five percent of them will become alcoholics and/or marry alcoholics.

And even though the recovery rate from alcoholism is very high (80 percent stay sober after treatment) — only thirty out of thirty-four people ever reach treatment.

The rest eventually go insane or die from one of the 350 secondary disease/disorders to alcoholism.

Don't these women ask for help? Yes, they do. Just like the woman you just read about, there are masses of bright, articulate women who regularly see mental-health professionals. Women constitute at least 75 percent of the total patient load in this country.

Unfortunately, many therapists view them as "sensitive," "emotionally-vulnerable," "character-disordered" people who need to take pills to get through life. The pills, especially, are seen as part of the solution, rather than as they are — part of the problem.

Therapists often do not want to "call" someone an alcoholic, an addict, even though the A.M.A. says that it is a disease. This stigma is killing millions of adult daughters of alcoholics in therapy, today.

Write your feelings and thoughts on the following four comments, concerning the chapter you just read:

1.) This behavior felt 'glamorous' when I drank; and shameful when I got sober.

2.) I never looked at this behavior as if it were "stealing".

3.)   If it's *me* who wants *your* husband, I only care about *me*. If it's *my* husband, I hate *you*. I know I'm inconsistent.

4.)   I never like to think about consequences.

Draw a circle or a square or a rectangle for yourself, for your married lover, for his or her wife. Name the shapes. Place a one-word description in each of the shapes.

What feelings can you identify in each of the shapes? For one moment, try to "get into the skin" of each of the parties involved. What are the feelings?

Write the phrases that you could "hear" your parent (s) say, if he or she were responding to this chapter: _____

_____

_____

_____

How do these phrases of your parent (s) still evoke reactions in you today? _____

_____

_____

_____

If your spouse, boyfriend, girlfriend, etc., were to read this chapter, given the history of your relationship, what do you believe would be his or her response? _____

_____

How do you feel about that probable response? _____

_____

Do you think you would encounter uncomfortable feelings if you would share your innermost thoughts and feelings about this chapter with your closest loved one?

_____

_____

_____

Do you feel there is any way to begin open communication with your closest loved one about the feelings you just expressed? Is there a way to begin discussion about your feelings honestly, without making yourself too vulnerable? (and in a way in which that person could really *hear* you?) _____

_____

_____

_____

_____

_____

_____

_____

What subjects come to your mind as you read this chapter? What subjects do you believe are necessary to deal with, at some time (today or in the future), to continue your own healing?

_____

_____

_____

_____

_____

_____

After reading this chapter, what area of difficulty arises in your mind—an area that brings up emotional pain, when you try to change your attitude toward it, or change your life-style concerning that area? _____

_____

_____

_____

_____

_____

_____

_____

How can you lessen the pain that you anticipated in the above question? Can you do so by lowering your expectations of yourself? Can you anticipate taking a beginning *very* small step to change, instead of big ones? Can you allow yourself times of rest, of break, between changes? Do you have a spiritual program of recovery that buffers the pain surrounding this issue?_____

_____

_____

_____

_____

_____

_____

Belief systems can either increase or decrease psychic pain. What are your intrinsic beliefs about the ideas presented in this chapter? Do they dovetail with what you were taught as a child? Are they ideas that protected you as a child, but that hinder your growth as an ethical adult? _____

_____

_____

_____

_____

_____

_____

What are your beliefs about the higher power? Do you think that God is basically a punishing God? If you felt fear when dealing with the questions at the end of this chapter, does this at all have to do with a concept of a punishing God? _____

_____

_____

_____

_____

_____

_____

List positive change (s) you have already made in your life, concerning the issue (s) in this chapter and how they have affected you. _____

_____

_____

_____

_____

Describe the details — the actual emotional steps —of your journey to reach this more comfortable state that you talked about in the previous question. _____

_____

_____

_____

_____

How may you learn from this journey, to face other situations in life that seem difficult, but that are opportunities for growth? _____

_____

_____

_____

Have you had any losses, any setbacks, around any of the issues in this chapter? Have you had times when you felt you were "going backwards," not growing, even though you were trying to get through a difficult situation? Were there times when you felt like staying in a sick situation, and not trying to grow at all? When you liked it the way it was?_____

_____

_____

_____

_____

_____

_____

Having come through this, and faced it somehow, do you see growth, perhaps despite yourself? _____

_____

_____

_____

_____

_____

_____

Replacing
the Excitement
of Sickness

"Give thanks to the Lord Almighty, for the Lord is good; His love endures forever" (Jer. 33:11).

5

"I was so unaware of what I was really like. I fell in love with so many people, so often, and yet I thought I was very, very selective.

"When I was drinking, my 'loves' were puppy loves, teenager loves. I'm more selective now. I don't fall in love because her hair is thick with the highlights of gold I love, and she moves a certain way. I *like* it, but I don't go ape over it like I once did!

"I love her today, but she's not a goddess! Now, she's a woman. Flawed. Good. Wonderful. Not so wonderful. Fine. Okay. In between. Human. There did not used to be any in-betweens. I wasn't 'in love' before. I 'loved' the outer layer of the onion. That's all. And not even the whole outer layer! Maybe just the gleam in her eye! That's it! Nothing else! How long can that last?! Even *I* would get bored with that!" Peter laughed.

This thirty-five-year-old was the first person I spoke with. The next to describe his experience was Sam, the 'recovered-Catholic' (his words) — who formerly was hard on himself and is now able to twinkle at his shortcomings. (They have less impact, for that.)

Listen to my interview with Sam: "They often say to the newcomer in recovery who is falling in love every week with a new person, 'ALCOHOLICS DON'T FALL IN LOVE, THEY FALL IN LUST.' Don't some people deny this — don't they think it's always 'love?' Did you go through this?" I asked.

"As far back as I can remember, I felt great lust even when I was a child. But the strong Catholic upbringing I had made me go into denial about this and call it 'love.'"

"Did you *really* believe it was love, and just agreed that it was 'lust' — without really thinking it through?" I asked.

"Back when I was drinking, and even way before I started drinking, I felt absolutely in love all the time. I got so totally involved, immersed, infatuated with someone else, it was like I only saw the sheer beauty of this person.

When I was near her or close by, I saw none of her faults. None. It went from that to sex, or lust, or whatever you call it. I felt that that was the ideal. That's why I couldn't go to prostitutes. I had to *love* a person.

"Maybe what I mean by saying I lusted, even though I was always in love (which seems like a contradiction), is that I obsessively *had* to have this person — to possess her — no matter what the consequences to her, to me, to her husband — to anyone!

"When I became attracted to a woman — I guess it was chemistry — I became obsessed with meeting and possessing, and having sex with that person. I would meet a woman who was from D.C., and I lived in Atlanta. I'd wind up chasing her to D.C., and I didn't even know her name — but I did it — *I wanted that woman* and I would go to any lengths to possess her.

"I did the same thing with another woman I met in Atlantic City: I followed her all the way to St Louis, Missouri, only to wind up totally devastated because nothing happened when I got there!

"When I am attracted to a person, that's *it*. I love that person on sight.

"Of course, if I wound up with that person in a party, say, and happened to have a long conversation with her, I was likely to lose interest in her in just a few minutes. She was this ideal *if I knew nothing about her.* But if she fell short of it, that was it. It was over. Done.

"When I was drinking, I would climb a fire escape just to spend a few minutes with the object of my love. It was like a cinemascope existence. Everything was grand. A grand scale. Marvelous or terrible. I would do very insane things just to get to that person.

"I lived on raw emotions. Of course, all this led me to be very possessive. And that always leads to getting hurt. At least, it did for me. So, I usually wound up plunged into despair. Until the next 'love.'

"I never learned from my experiences. I tried, but I couldn't. I *never* thought, at the height of a new love, that I was setting myself up for a big letdown.

"Maybe it's like what I've heard from people: *If a parking meter paid attention to an alcoholic, he'd fall madly in love with it!* That was me. Look at me in 'that way,' combined with a kind of chemistry — and that's it! If the chemistry was 'sort of' there, but if she paid absolutely no attention to me, repeatedly — the feeling would fade. I would become resentful and depressed for a while.

. "The only problem with the excitement of fantasy is that it doesn't work: other people are going to be themselves and not the way I want them to be! *And that never occurred to me!* I dreaded it — I thought about it and quickly dismissed it — but I didn't really think that that would happen on a regular basis!"

I thought about my conversations. I wonder; do we, perhaps, call it 'lust' when it is a surface attraction? Does it turn into 'love' if we continue to be attracted to that person after we know them better? What about people who stay with abuse? Do certain idealists feel that the people who stay when they are battered are 'virtuous' and 'truly those who love' — as opposed to surface-communicators? If one is unable to know how to love because one was raised in a terribly violent home-life, is it better to abstain from relationships until one knows how to love? Does a certain amount of reasonable discretion preclude 'lust'?

I feel that all the questions that occurred to me involved me trying to ask others to define *their* terms, for *themselves*.

Without knowing *our* sense of what 'love' and 'lust' means —without being able to place these in our value systems — we cannot make wise choices or even know what's going on with us. And I cannot grow until I know what I am about: what I do; why I do what I do with others; whether I hurt from it or am at peace; whether I believe the pain of change is more painful than the pain of inertia.

"When I got sober, I was able to begin to adapt to, and accept, another person's persona — more than I could when I took pills or drank. I could begin to still love them when I saw their faults. I could still be attracted to them.

"Then, after a certain long relationship (for me), with a lot of love, I felt like I was being eased out. I started getting paranoid and believing she was seeing someone else when she wasn't. I started getting depressed because I could not have my own way.

"I felt I had been dumped. It was a tremendous blow to my ego. It hurts. I tried hard, then, to accept reality. I worked hard to get back into the normal routine I had before I met her.

"It seems that it is true that alcoholics don't have relationships. *We take hostages!* For *this* alcoholic, anyway, that's what broke us up. She couldn't take it. But this program of A.A. helped me to recover from that depression rather quickly. A.A. people loved me until I could love myself again.

"It was a big revelation to sit in an A.A. meeting and hear a man tell my story: he had the same experiences I did. But he came to the realization that he wanted a woman who would want what *he* wanted. His fantasy did not at all include what *she* wanted! It didn't even occur to him to think she may want a different kind of relating! And if she did, tough!

"I don't know about you, but if I had to have the attitude of 'what can I do for you' rather than 'what can you do for me' — that would be the end of *that* fantasy!

"My fantasies could *only* be self-centered. And my sobriety demanded that I become less self-centered in *all* the areas of my life. I just kept coming back to A.A. and I got better despite myself. I didn't have to force it. If I had tried to, I would've gotten depressed. I would have felt the loss of excitement too heavily. It seemed like it just got *eased* away."

—John C.

When I asked people how they 'got over' the pursuance of the unobtainable and/or the depression of not getting what they wanted (i.e., the excitement of sickness), I was not expecting such a simple, yet so powerful solution. The A.A. 'Big Book' (as it is fondly called) says that one of alcoholics' main problems is 'self-centered fear.' And the solution presented is simple, yet difficult: get out of Self. Get involved in helping another person; get involved in thinking about what other people want and need; get aware that one is not the center of the universe, not even the center of one's spouse's universe!

David has a similar story:

"I lived in New Orleans. I had absolutely unlimited funds. I had limos and huge expense accounts. At the same time, I wanted to commit suicide and couldn't. Sex had gotten to the point where it meant nothing. I couldn't function as a human being, much less sexually. Nothing appealed to me. People who knew me (but who didn't really) thought I was the most ungrateful, most unappreciative person on the face of the earth. Here, I had everything. Friends would take me out to try to cheer me up. They would take me to fine restaurants, marvelous museums. I was in a shell. I didn't want to be there with them. My father was a judge; I came from a wealthy family. I had a huge inheritance from my grandparents. My wife is Austrian, and an accomplished pianist. My children are wonderful. I had it all and I couldn't feel anything but numb.

"As my alcoholism progressed, I would increasingly do things that went against my own values. But as soon as I would do one of these things — my womanizing, my having sex with anything and anybody that came along, to get a momentary high away from my growing chronic depression — I would , for a little while, be appalled at myself, and then I would internalize that behavior and it would become a part of me. It would no longer be alien. In that slow and insidious way, I lost my own sense of values.

"Sometimes, my behavior frightened me. I would *hope* that the alcohol got me into a situation. I hoped it wasn't because I was actually developing into what I saw as a weird, depraved freak. I felt so ashamed. But I continued.

"I wound up beating myself with chains, not because I got a kick out of it, but because it hurt and I thought I could beat this sickness out of me.

"I felt so emotionally depressed that I needed the high from pure lust. Of course, I couldn't deal with people on any level anyway, by that time. The only thing I hadn't sunk to, it seemed, was doing it for money. I wouldn't have sex for money nor would I marry for money. It was all that was left of my former value system.

"Sex is a part of my life, now. It doesn't rule my life any more than alcohol does, now.

"It took about five years or more of sobriety for me to come to terms with my values and become contented with sex and life in a comfortable way.

"I had to become *willing* to think a different way about people. And be willing to change. I couldn't force it; it had to happen in a slow way. But I had to be willing. I had to become willing to adjust more to life, instead of having it always adjust to me. As I became more tolerant and more caring about people, generally, I think it naturally followed that in my sex life, these new attitudes crept in there too.

"When I thought about excitement, before, it was what *I* wanted! It did not matter what *you* wanted. You can't go after excitement in the determined way I did without it becoming a ruthless pursuit of *'I want what I want no matter what the consequences are to anyone else.'*

"When I began to incorporate a more caring way of life into my attitudes, I couldn't compartmentalize my sex life — not without alcohol or pills in me. I naturally became less able to be loving in one area of my life, and rotten in another."

None of these interviews had a 'magic zapper' answer. But they had answers. And they had hope and they provide hope. The process of slowly shedding that skin of 'Self Will Run Riot' is *hard*. It causes resentment. It causes depression.

But just knowing that all those people you've met in A.A. who stayed around long enough to get the benefits, *are* having fun — is enough to keep one coming back. One 'fun-loving' guy told me that he only trusted that he'd be happy after he saw some *real* 'fun lovers' he 'knew from before' who were just as happy-looking sober as they *used to* look. "But they also looked smarter," he told me. "They don't get into dumb situations. They're savvy now. Happy, too."

Write your feelings and thoughts on the following four comments, concerning the chapter you just read:

1.)   I don't quite trust that I can be happy if I give up excited misery.

2.)   I get depressed when I read that fantasy doesn't work.

3.) I never really thought too much about the fact that I don't see people as being three-dimensional. Not if they are people I am attracted to.

4.) It never occurred to me that my wanting excitement might be tied - in with my self-centeredness.

Draw circles (representing yourself) somewhere on each spectrum:

Boredom	Contentment

Confusion	Clarity

Self-deception	Self-honesty

Unable to see change as beneficial	Ability to be openminded and flexible

Write the phrases that you could "hear" your parent (s) say, if he or she were responding to this chapter: _____

_____

_____

_____

How do these phrases of your parent (s) still evoke reactions in you today? _____

_____

_____

_____

If your spouse, boyfriend, girlfriend, etc., were to read this chapter, given the history of your relationship, what do you believe would be his or her response? _____

_____

How do you feel about that probable response? _____

_____

Do you think you would encounter uncomfortable feelings if you would share your innermost thoughts and feelings about this chapter with your closest loved one?

_____

_____

_____

Do you feel there is any way to begin open communication with your closest loved one about the feelings you just expressed? Is there a way to begin discussion about your feelings honestly, without making yourself too vulnerable? (and in a way in which that person could really *hear* you?) _____

_____

_____

_____

_____

_____

_____

_____

What subjects come to your mind as you read this chapter? What subjects do you believe are necessary to deal with, at some time (today or in the future), to continue your own healing?

_____

_____

_____

_____

_____

_____

After reading this chapter, what area of difficulty arises in your mind—an area that brings up emotional pain, when you try to change your attitude toward it, or change your life-style concerning that area? _____

_____

_____

_____

_____

_____

_____

_____

How can you lessen the pain that you anticipated in the above question? Can you do so by lowering your expectations of yourself? Can you anticipate taking a beginning *very* small step to change, instead of big ones? Can you allow yourself times of rest, of break, between changes? Do you have a spiritual program of recovery that buffers the pain surrounding this issue?_____

_____

_____

_____

_____

_____

_____

Belief systems can either increase or decrease psychic pain. What are your intrinsic beliefs about the ideas presented in this chapter? Do they dovetail with what you were taught as a child? Are they ideas that protected you as a child, but that hinder your growth as an ethical adult? _____

_____

_____

_____

_____

_____

_____

What are your beliefs about the higher power? Do you think that God is basically a punishing God? If you felt fear when dealing with the questions at the end of this chapter, does this at all have to do with a concept of a punishing God? _____

_____

_____

_____

_____

_____

_____

List positive change (s) you have already made in your life, concerning the issue (s) in this chapter and how they have affected you. _____

_____

_____

_____

_____

Describe the details — the actual emotional steps —of your journey to reach this more comfortable state that you talked about in the previous question. _____

_____

_____

_____

_____

_____

How may you learn from this journey, to face other situations in life that seem difficult, but that are opportunities for growth? _____

_____

_____

_____

Have you had any losses, any setbacks, around any of the issues in this chapter? Have you had times when you felt you were "going backwards," not growing, even though you were trying to get through a difficult situation? Were there times when you felt like staying in a sick situation, and not trying to grow at all? When you liked it the way it was?_____

_____

_____

_____

_____

_____

_____

Having come through this, and faced it somehow, do you see growth, perhaps despite yourself? _____

_____

_____

_____

_____

_____

_____

_____

AIDS: Families of Alcoholics — Hidden High-Risk Group?

"Peace I leave with you; my peace give I unto you. I do not give to you as the world gives. Do not let your hearts be troubled and do not be afraid" (John 14:27).

6

While on a lecture tour in California, I led a short-term couples group. The group was somewhat unique in that the couples had few remaining secrets from their pasts.

Bob C. recounted: "I was at one of those California parties where everyone was on pot and booze and cocaine. I wound up with a woman. I was in a blackout. I woke up the next morning on the sofa, in her huge sitting room, and heard the water running in the bathroom. I went in and saw my 'girl' in her boxer shorts, shaving!"

Most of the people in the room burst out laughing —except his wife. Doing a real quick arithmetical function, she realized that that business trip of his was only as far back as 1985. AIDS was widespread. This was California. Lots of gays had been infected.

She didn't know whether she was more mortified because he hadn't told her and she had to find out about it in this group, or whether she had to digest yet another sexual encounter of his, or whether she possibly now had to deal with the fact that *she* might have AIDS because of what happened. It didn't matter if he "didn't know it," which is what she knew he was going to hammer at her to make her feel guilty for blaming him.

And it was so easy to make her feel guilty.

How do you ask your husband (or wife) to get a blood test after he or she was out all night drinking, when you're even too scared to bring in pizza and not cook one night?

How do you ask your loved one to get a blood test when you are still in denial about the sexual life of your partner?

How do you ask your loved one to get a blood test when your denial about alcoholism is compounded by the general denial concerning the spread of AIDS among heterosexuals?

"IT CAN'T HAPPEN TO ME!"

And we haven't even touched on the topic of alcoholics and incest. What do we say to the non-alcoholic parent who sees alcoholism and yet does not 'see' the incest perpetrated on her child or children. Incest is bad enough; what about the three-year-old or eighteen-month-old who may be getting fatally infected?

Alcoholics who would not have sex with female prostitutes while sober, can find themselves in such situations, drunk. Eighty percent of female prostitutes are heavy drug users, and thirty-five percent of AIDS cases are i.v. drug users. Sixty-one percent of i.v. users are infected with the AIDS virus.

Drinking alcoholics are vulnerable to experiment with injectable drugs because judgment is impaired — even if that same action would horrify them, were they sober.

Alcoholics have regular blackouts. Alcoholics who are essentially heterosexual can fall prey to male prostitutes who need drug money, and who use hidden paraphernalia to appear to be female. This often works with people who are drunk and whose vision and perception are impaired. If in a blackout, the alcoholic often does not remember this at all.

There is a minority group in recovery from alcoholism that has yet to be acknowledged: the married men who love their wives, but are "closet" homosexuals. Not viewing this in a judgmental way, we're seeing several more layers of denial on top of the alcoholism and AIDS denials: he doesn't want to tell his wife he is homosexual or bisexual — or that he once was, while drinking.

The wife may have unconsciously noticed his body language and quickly dismissed it. Who wants to admit to herself that she married a man who may prefer men over her?

She's having a hard enough time dealing with his *alcoholism*! And if he's in A.A. and recovered, she and he both want to believe that the past "is all over with." She doesn't want to be accused of "bringing up the past again and not really having forgiven him for his past sex life." He glares at her and hisses, "What NOW?! You never stop, do you?!"

Like many recovering alcoholics who mouth the word "disease," he doesn't really believe his past life can ever be looked at in any way other than moral. He can't stop judging himself for the past.

He doesn't see alcoholism *or* AIDS as a diagnosis, but as an accusation.

I interviewed many alcoholics, spouses of alcoholics, adult children, and parents of alcoholics about this issue.

I threw some questions and ideas out to the groups:

(1). Do you diminish the idea that AIDS may become or is a problem, since some of you live in small towns seemingly forgotten by the 'big world' out there?

(2). Do you agree that "there is no wrong way to ask your spouse to get tested?" One woman told me that she was afraid to suggest that she was really afraid he may have AIDS. So, she said she was concerned about *herself* since her surgery and transfusion — so why didn't he come along and get tested too? He told her that *he* had not had surgery!

She thought fast and said, "Look, the blood donor was my sister, but who knows about her? You want to find out for yourself if you caught it from me!" Despite his protests, he went for the test.

Sometimes, the only way a worried spouse of a drinking alcoholic can get her husband to be tested is through 'subterfuge.' I see nothing wrong with that. If she attends Al-Anon for long enough, she will eventually, like everyone else there, get enough self-esteem to face life in an upfront manner. For now, though, let's let her live long enough to reach that stage. (It's similar to this analogy: many Al-Anon members suggest to spouses of alcoholics who are afraid to tell their husbands that they are going to Al-Anon, to tell them they are going to a church meeting. It's true — the meetings are usually held in churches. Inevitably, the spouse reaches the point where telling the truth about where she is going is as easy as water rolling off a duck's back.)

(3). Are you in a situation, now, where you are dating a recovering alcoholic who was recently drinking (1979 was when the first AIDS cases were discovered)? And even if (s)he has been sober during the entire AIDS epidemic, are you sure that person has not had sex with anyone except yourself?

How do you feel and think about all this? Do you have any idea how you might handle this —or ignore it?

(4). If you feel you *cannot* bring yourself to deal with yet another issue in alcoholism — do you allow yourself to "put this issue on the shelf to, yes, deal with it later?" How do you see yourself possibly dealing with this later?

BETTY: "I don't want to tackle dealing with *anything* else. I mean, it's just starting to calm down in my house since sobriety. It's really starting to be nice, and we're on our way to a vacation for the first time and it's wonderful. It's like 'stirring up stuff.' What he might have done while we were going through all our problems five, six years ago — I don't want to bring it up again. But, he'll think I'm bringing it up again if I ask him to get tested for AIDS because there's a long incubation period for this thing. God knows what went on."

LAURA: "My husband had been in a treatment center, had been in a hospital, had been tested. I asked him directly. I just asked him straight out. Because I wasn't worried that he'd get mad. I don't know why, I just wasn't. I just asked him. I said, 'With all the AIDS business going around, do you think you were ever intimate with anyone during that period?' First, I told him why. He said he had been hospitalized and he had been given every test known to man, and he knew from that point on. He never did say if he had been before, which is fine. I don't care. He could say yes or no. The point is, was he tested? Which he was. So, that was *it* for me. And, I know my husband. I know that if he's not drinking, I know how he behaves. I just know he's not been with anyone else. Because if he was, he would tell me. And probably brag. I mean, I *know* him."

MARGE:"Anybody new to Al-Anon probably could not talk about it. Most new persons, given the kind of personalities that the families generally have —you know, everything's a secret — that's one of the biggest symptoms of the relationship. I know how it is in my family. I *still* don't trust. Not *entirely*. I never will. When you first come in for family treatment, you can't even face something like that, I don't think. If your greatest fear would be illness, and AIDS happened to be one of the illnesses you were obsessing on, sure, you might face that, but that's normally the *last* thing. You want to know how to get your husband sober. It's that simple. But, after Al-Anon, you can't ignore forever, you can't deny forever, no matter what the subject. You get too uncomfortable not facing things. I think you *know* you're recovering when you can *face* things. Prior to then, it's not like you don't *want* to face; you *can't*. You just *can't*. Once you've gotten that (whatever it is) that comes from going to meetings and being told you're okay, and you learn to live just for today, and not worry about all the wrongs you did in the past or what's going to happen in the future, you do start having a few good days. You start to be able to face things. Before, everything had a bad ending. And you couldn't cope with anything, anyway. So it was automatic that everything would have a bad ending. The alcoholism was going to outwit you. And what was the point of bringing up anything of substance? You knew it would be either ignored or laughed at. 'You're making something out of nothing. You see an alcoholic everywhere —.' "

BETTY: "Given I'm the kind of person I am, I won't talk about things. If I suspected he might have been in contact with AIDS, I would get tested on the sly. I would just go by myself. If I didn't have it, I would hope it meant that he didn't have it."

MARGE:"It seems to me that since the issue is life and death, as AIDS is, I would think you would face it the same way you would face violence. How do you face violence? You eventually *do* face it. A person coming into a program of recovery may be battered, but I'll bet that if they are in there any length of time, they are not going to be battered any more. Because they are going to grow so much that they *cannot* and *will not* accept it. It *is* unacceptable behavior. It would be the same with AIDS. Regardless of whether you are afraid you are going to be abandoned by the alcoholic or not, you *say* something. The fear of AIDS is so much more *immediate* than alcoholism."

BETTY: "I would not sleep with the man. I wouldn't. I might be afraid to bring up talking about AIDS, but I'm afraid of AIDS more than I'm afraid of my alcoholic! I don't want to get it. No one is worth that kind of dying. I might die spiritually from living with alcoholism, but don't give me AIDS, you know?!"

Write your feelings and thoughts on the following four comments, concerning the chapter you just read:

1.)   I'm so scared to deal with the thought of AIDS, it was hard even to read this chapter.

2.)   I'm starting to face the fact that my husband is alcoholic. I feel angry and overwhelmed with fear that I have to look at the possibility that he may have AIDS, too.

3.)   I can't seem to make myself stop worrying, and yet I don't know how to begin to get the courage to *find out*.

4.)   This can't happen to *me*.

Draw a circle with the word "fear" in it. Draw a circle with you in it.

How large is the fear circle? How large is the lettering for the word "Fear?" How large is the circle with you in it? Is it as large as the fear-circle? How close are they?

Write the phrases that you could "hear" your parent (s) say, if he or she were responding to this chapter: _____

_____

_____

_____

How do these phrases of your parent (s) still evoke reactions in you today? _____

_____

_____

_____

If your spouse, boyfriend, girlfriend, etc., were to read this chapter, given the history of your relationship, what do you believe would be his or her response? _____

_____

How do you feel about that probable response? _____

_____

Do you think you would encounter uncomfortable feelings if you would share your innermost thoughts and feelings about this chapter with your closest loved one?

_____

_____

_____

Do you feel there is any way to begin open communication with your closest loved one about the feelings you just expressed? Is there a way to begin discussion about your feelings honestly, without making yourself too vulnerable? (and in a way in which that person could really *hear* you?) _____

_____

_____

_____

_____

_____

_____

_____

What subjects come to your mind as you read this chapter? What subjects do you believe are necessary to deal with, at some time (today or in the future), to continue your own healing?

_____

_____

_____

_____

_____

_____

After reading this chapter, what area of difficulty arises in your mind—an area that brings up emotional pain, when you try to change your attitude toward it, or change your life-style concerning that area? _____

_____

_____

_____

_____

_____

_____

How can you lessen the pain that you anticipated in the above question? Can you do so by lowering your expectations of yourself? Can you anticipate taking a beginning *very* small step to change, instead of big ones? Can you allow yourself times of rest, of break, between changes? Do you have a spiritual program of recovery that buffers the pain surrounding this issue?_____

_____

_____

_____

_____

_____

_____

Belief systems can either increase or decrease psychic pain. What are your intrinsic beliefs about the ideas presented in this chapter? Do they dovetail with what you were taught as a child? Are they ideas that protected you as a child, but that hinder your growth as an ethical adult? _____

_____

_____

_____

_____

_____

_____

What are your beliefs about the higher power? Do you think that God is basically a punishing God? If you felt fear when dealing with the questions at the end of this chapter, does this at all have to do with a concept of a punishing God? _____

_____

_____

_____

_____

_____

_____

List positive change (s) you have already made in your life, concerning the issue (s) in this chapter and how they have affected you. _____

_____

_____

_____

_____

_____

Describe the details — the actual emotional steps —of your journey to reach this more comfortable state that you talked about in the previous question. _____

_____

_____

_____

_____

_____

_____

How may you learn from this journey, to face other situations in life that seem difficult, but that are opportunities for growth? _____

_____

_____

_____

Have you had any losses, any setbacks, around any of the issues in this chapter? Have you had times when you felt you were "going backwards," not growing, even though you were trying to get through a difficult situation? Were there times when you felt like staying in a sick situation, and not trying to grow at all? When you liked it the way it was?_____

_____

_____

_____

_____

_____

_____

Having come through this, and faced it somehow, do you see growth, perhaps despite yourself? _____

_____

_____

_____

_____

_____

_____

_____

Notes to
Family Counselors
and Their Clients

"The fruit of the Spirit is love, joy, peace, patience, kindness, goodness, faithfulness, gentleness and self-control" (Gal. 5:22).

7

Most of the problems we have talked about in this book are so very treatable. However, I think it is just about totally useless to do marital counseling with a couple if one of them is a *drinking* alcoholic. The alcoholic can have all the good intentions in the world, but all those good intentions go flying out the window with the next drink.

Another factor that contributes to a lack of success in counseling drinking alcoholics is the fact that alcoholism is a progressive disease. Every day the alcoholic is drinking, the disease is progressing; and every day the alcoholic is drinking, he or she is daily becoming less able to cope with the realities of life or with the intimacies of the marital relationship.

In addition, alcoholism necessitates a life-style of blame. The alcoholic, driven by the alcoholism, needs to blame others and situations for his or her drinking, in order to continue the drinking. Many alcoholics do not wish to go to a counseling session "smelling of booze." So he goes, needing a drink, and in a state of withdrawal. This withdrawal often manifests itself as a general anxiety, a general agitation.

This agitation causes anger, and it seems to be usually explained by the alcoholic as, "I'm angry because —" (pointing out some possibly otherwise-minor problem in the relationship). The *alcoholism* forces the alcoholic to blame his agitation on the marriage rather than on the alcoholism.

Furthermore, early-stage alcoholism is often relatively nondetectable, almost always only manifesting with psychological symptoms. Therefore, many therapists see only the psychological problems, and think that this is a "psychological problem," rather than an alcoholism problem.

To get at the truth of the matter, I think it is important for the counselor to obtain a thorough alcoholism history of both sides of the family. Then start asking about each person's drinking. Then, ask the *other* person about the other person's drinking. If there are children in the family, ask them about the drinking in the family. It usually does not help to say, "Do you think that your husband, or your father, or your mother, or your wife is an alcoholic?" Many people are reluctant to "label" somebody. They think that one has to be in a late stage of alcoholism, before one can 'name it.' Also, they don't recognize the disease. If you ask the question differently, you often get a straight answer about whether there is or isn't a drinking problem. Some questions that one can ask are, "Does this person's drinking ever bother you?" or "Do you get uncomfortable about that person's drinking?"

I would also ask the person who you are questioning about their own drinking — if they have ever 'switched' to a lighter drink.

'Switching' is usually a method of trying to control one's drinking, something that *non*-alcoholics don't need to do. One usually only tries to control one's drinking when one has a problem.

It is important to realize that the disease of alcoholism *forces* alcoholics to protect their drinking by lying about the amount and the frequency and duration of their drinking. It is not a moral judgment, it is a diagnosis, to say "This person lies about his drinking."

Let's now look at some of the 'games' that are often played out in counseling sessions, and that are often undetected by the counselor who is either: (a) unskilled in seeing alcoholism symptoms and the games that manifest from the alcoholism in the therapy office, or (b) himself or herself an adult child of an alcoholic who is easily baffled by the proceedings and the twists and turns that go on in counseling sessions with these clients.

Glenda and Timothy are the parents of Tommy, a seventeen-year-old who is "acting out." That's why they "took him to see a therapist."

The therapist was a highly-skilled professional marriage and family counselor in California who had been in practice for twenty-five years.

It was a case of undetected family alcoholism. The child was in the early stages of addiction (which could have been detected had a thorough family history been taken. The son's grandfather and great-grandfather were alcoholics. Grandchildren of alcoholics are at high risk.) In addition, the father of the child was an untreated alcoholic. He was not drinking for the last two years, but his *alcoholism* was untreated. He did not attend A.A., or any treatment to deal with his alcoholism, and he thought he could deal with it all by himself. So, his behavior did not change — except that he put down the bottle.

The counselor saw the child alone, saw the family together, and saw the parents as a couple. This went on for a few months, and, in one of the couple's sessions, the mother brought up some changes that she would like to see in the family. They had been discussed by her and the therapist in several previous sessions when she was alone with the therapist. The therapist had agreed that these were reasonable goals that a family should aim towards. So, she brought these up in the couple's sessions.

Prior to this session, the father had also had individual sessions with the therapist. The therapist tried hard to get the father to "get in touch with his feelings." The therapist applauded the father so much that he allowed him to *talk* about his feelings, instead of requiring him to make *behavior* changes. His wife had to make *behavioral* changes; and the counseling became lopsided, as *she* had to perform more, and the husband was only required to *talk*.

The mother realized this and talked about her resentment. When this was pointed out to him, the therapist was surprised, and being a basically honest person, and meaning the best for his patients, he agreed with her. Even so, he seemed truly confused and expressed his bafflement at how this had all come about.

The alcoholic husband was a channel through which his alcoholism passed. The disease twisted situations in such a manner so that the alcoholic would not have to drop certain sick behaviors, enabling him to stay only "dry" (not "sober").

One could say, "This man was not drinking. He was an alcoholic but he was not drinking." Well, alcoholism is very patient. Even if an alcoholic is not drinking for a while, even for a few years, if the alcoholism is not treated, it will do its best to manipulate situations (through the alcoholic) to keep things as they are, to dis-allow the alcoholic to make significant changes towards healing, so that he is ripe, vulnerable, to return to drinking.

As it turned out, the therapist himself was an adult child of an alcoholic, who often found himself trying very hard to please his alcoholic clients, even if that meant twisting the therapy sessions around to suit the whims of the alcoholism. Of course, the counselor knew nothing of this. He was untreated for his family disease.

An even more-typical counseling fiasco that alcoholism can and does create is a scenario in which an alcoholic and spouse are the clients, and the spouse is angry and frustrated by the alcoholic's seemingly uncanny ability to 'shape up' in front of helping professionals. The alcoholic — male or female — 'turns on the charm' and the non-alcoholic spouse finds it very difficult to be believed, concerning the alcoholism. The non-alcoholic comes off as very overreactive, frustrated, inarticulate, and enraged.

The collusion that often results is that the alcoholic figuratively 'puts his arms around the shoulders' of the counselor and claims: "Now, you and I are fairly reasonable; *look* at this maniac I have to live with! Can't you see what I'm putting up with!" This usually makes the non-alcoholic (who has been through this before) feel sputteringly powerless, frustrated and angry; and she or he comes off as 'crazy.' The upshot is usually that the focus is taken off the alcoholism, and the therapy focuses on the "overreactive" spouse.

At that point, the *non-alcoholic* usually leaves counseling. (Or, if the counseling gets to the point where the counselor begins to *see through* the alcoholism, then the *alcoholic* drops out of counseling.)

The final result is often that, even though the non-alcoholic spouse came into the counseling in order to be able to increase the amount and intensity of love and intimacy in that family, after going through this professional stamp of approval that he or she really is crazy, this spouse winds up less able to trust the alcoholic than ever. (He was so powerful that he could actually con the counselor, even though the spouse couldn't express that because, "My Goodness! If I said that I would really seem crazy, wouldn't I?")

The non-alcoholic spouse crawls even further into the shell of self-protection and less intimacy.

And, everybody wonders why marriage counseling didn't work.

These are but a few of the 'games' that go on in counseling with undetected alcoholism. And what makes it even much more complicated is that so many adult children of alcoholics are going into the helping professions, and bringing with them not only the guilt and denial from their own families, but they also bring with them the *fear* of the alcoholic and an intense need to *please* alcoholics.

When the untreated counselor is manipulated by the alcoholism, I think the therapist is *not* consciously aware that he is a victim of the twists and turns of the *alcoholism*. I think he feels 'twinges,' he knows that he is not *leading* the couple, but following this couple in an uncomfortable 'grabbing the tiger by the tail,' so to speak, and trying to hold on for dear life while it runs rampant. He knows he is not somebody who can truly guide this couple, but he is baffled, and fearful of honesty.

And given the history of adult children of alcoholics (ACOAs), where all their formative lives were spent in denial about was was going on, and where they lied to themselves about the reality (because they had to in order to protect themselves), they bring these symptoms into the therapy sessions themselves.

They are not able to tell themselves what the uncomfortableness *is* in these sessions where they are not counseling, but 'holding on to a rampant tiger's tail.' They do not know how to stop this from going on. They just hope to God that it will get tired, and slow down, and they can take charge again.

Now, you may say to yourself, "Well, counselors usually go through a period where they have to 'get counseled' as part of their training. So, they are *not* untreated for their past."

Well, they are and they aren't. When they are going through therapy to learn to be counselors, they deal with a variety of problems from their pasts. But, almost none of these modalities takes into account the depth, bizarreness, and intensity of the denial, guilt, and fear that the child of an alcoholic brings into his or her adulthood.

A few years ago the NIAAA (National Institute of Alcohol Abuse and Alcoholism) conducted a study and discovered a startling fact. *Sixty percent of the freshman class at the University of Maryland's School of Medicine were first-born children of alcoholics.* I don't think it is an accident that adult children of alcoholics — with the bizarre guilt that they have grown up with — are literally self-driven towards the helping professions. They are trying to make some sense out of the nonsense they grew up with. But, when you don't realize it is futile to try to make sense out of a certain kind of nonsense, it is like chasing your tail all your life. You don't realize that you are desperately still trying to please your alcoholic parent, and this carries through to your alcoholic clients. But, you get angry because they are not grateful. Then you become guilty for feeling angry. Your vacillating feelings go from guilty to angry with your clients. You stay on the treadmill until you recognize that anger and its source. For, if the anger at alcoholics continues, so does your unconscious guilt that results from the anger. (You are still guilty for being angry at a 'sacred' parent!) Thus, the swing towards the guilt. And then, the lack of appreciation from the alcoholic (you are being nice again) brings back the anger. And the pendulum continues. Until you get help.

How many *untreated* ACOA-counselors are 'treating' families of alcoholics and therefore validating the disease patterns?

Write your feelings and thoughts on the following four comments, concerning the chapter you just read:

1.)   I never thought about the fact that when my alcoholic spouse is 'controlling' his drinking, he's probably in withdrawal.

2.)   I took my child to five counselors, and none of them saw the alcoholism. They assumed it was just a behavior problem.

3.)   I get so angry at my alcoholic husband that I scream at him in our counseling sessions. I *know* he's fooling the counselors. They think I'm exaggerating when I talk about alcoholism all the time. They think he drinks because of his marriage or his job. Then, they focus on my anger, instead of his drinking problem. They say he drinks because I am angry. They never answer me when I say I wasn't always angry when we first got married — not until he started staying out all night, drinking. They just chalk it all up to a 'lack of communication.'

4.)   I am an ACOA. I'm also a counselor. I certainly don't want to look at my parents' alcoholism, now. It's all behind me. I have a great career ahead of me. Yes, I'm still a little uneasy about all the things I don't want to look at. But, I've got it all together, now. All but a few things. Well, quite a few things. But, enough areas are fine. I really don't want any clients to run into me at ACOA meetings. Besides, the alcoholism was my parents' problem. It's *not* mine. Yeah, I know these things have their lasting effect. Well, I'm too busy living in the present.

Draw three circles, one of you, one of your spouse, one of your counselor. Name those circles. Write in one word that describes each.

Now draw two circles, one representing you, and one representing your spouse, as you are now, when alone.

Now draw two circles, of you and your spouse, again; this time, draw the two of you as you were, before you entered counseling. Examine the relative sizes of the circles in relation to one another. Do the circles have equal "strength?" How close are they?

Write the phrases that you could "hear" your parent (s) say, if he or she were responding to this chapter: _____

_____

_____

_____

How do these phrases of your parent (s) still evoke reactions in you today? _____

_____

_____

_____

If your spouse, boyfriend, girlfriend, etc., were to read this chapter, given the history of your relationship, what do you believe would be his or her response? _____

_____

How do you feel about that probable response? _____

_____

Do you think you would encounter uncomfortable feelings if you would share your innermost thoughts and feelings about this chapter with your closest loved one?

_____

_____

_____

Do you feel there is any way to begin open communication with your closest loved one about the feelings you just expressed? Is there a way to begin discussion about your feelings honestly, without making yourself too vulnerable? (and in a way in which that person could really *hear* you?) _____

_____

_____

_____

_____

_____

_____

_____

What subjects come to your mind as you read this chapter? What subjects do you believe are necessary to deal with, at some time (today or in the future), to continue your own healing?

_____

_____

_____

_____

_____

_____

_____

After reading this chapter, what area of difficulty arises in your mind—an area that brings up emotional pain, when you try to change your attitude toward it, or change your life-style concerning that area? _____

_____

_____

_____

_____

_____

_____

_____

How can you lessen the pain that you anticipated in the above question? Can you do so by lowering your expectations of yourself? Can you anticipate taking a beginning *very* small step to change, instead of big ones? Can you allow yourself times of rest, of break, between changes? Do you have a spiritual program of recovery that buffers the pain surrounding this issue?_____

_____

_____

_____

_____

_____

_____

Belief systems can either increase or decrease psychic pain. What are your intrinsic beliefs about the ideas presented in this chapter? Do they dovetail with what you were taught as a child? Are they ideas that protected you as a child, but that hinder your growth as an ethical adult? _____

_____

_____

_____

_____

_____

_____

What are your beliefs about the higher power? Do you think that God is basically a punishing God? If you felt fear when dealing with the questions at the end of this chapter, does this at all have to do with a concept of a punishing God? _____

_____

_____

_____

_____

_____

_____

List positive change (s) you have already made in your life, concerning the issue (s) in this chapter and how they have affected you. _____

_____

_____

_____

_____

_____

Describe the details — the actual emotional steps —of your journey to reach this more comfortable state that you talked about in the previous question. _____

_____

_____

_____

_____

_____

How may you learn from this journey, to face other situations in life that seem difficult, but that are opportunities for growth? _____

_____

_____

_____

Have you had any losses, any setbacks, around any of the issues in this chapter? Have you had times when you felt you were "going backwards," not growing, even though you were trying to get through a difficult situation? Were there times when you felt like staying in a sick situation, and not trying to grow at all? When you liked it the way it was?_____

_____

_____

_____

_____

_____

Having come through this, and faced it somehow, do you see growth, perhaps despite yourself? _____

_____

_____

_____

_____

_____

_____

Recovery Directory

MORE BOOKS FROM TOBY RICE DREWS:

1.) *Getting Your Children Sober* $7.95
2.) *Light This Day!* (Daily Meditations/Daily Journal)
$7.95
3.) *Getting Them Sober,* Volume One $3.95
4.) *Getting Them Sober,* Volume Two $3.95
5.) *Getting Them Sober,* Volume Three $3.95
6.) *Get Rid of Anxiety and Stress* $4.95

These books can either be ordered through your local bookstore, or can be mail-ordered, by sending in the coupon below.

Please tear off and mail in this coupon with your filled-out order, plus payment and $1.50 per order for postage and handling. Send to: Recovery Communications, Inc. — P.O. Box 19910 — Baltimore, Maryland 21211

Books Ordered:
Quantity   Title

_____

_____

_____

_____

Your name_____
Mailing Address_____
City, State, Zip _____

"Our Family"

AUDIO/VIDEO/FILMS

• "Counseling for Families of Alcoholics" an 8-audiocassette album with Study Guide .. over 200 minutes w/ Toby Drews: reg. $80—special $39.95

• Brand New: "Getting Your Children Sober", the video $395

— disposable preview: $35 —

preview price deductible from purchase fee

• no time-limit for preview!
• no need to return it
• a short collage/sampling of the actual video

• "GETTING THEM SOBER", the 16 mm film, $395 SALE
(reg. $625)

the video: $295
rental/preview: $50
(preview avail. in film format only)

Mail in this coupon with your order: Payment or organizational-purchase-order must accompany all orders. Please send to: Recovery Communications, Inc., P.O. Box 19910, Baltimore, Maryland 21211

Name _____

Mailing Address_____

City, State, Zip _____

Area Code, Phone ( ) _____

Audio, Video, and/or Film order: _____

_____

164